Spirit IN WHOLENESS

The Spiritual Path to Healing and Wholeness

MARY WEBB EDLUND

Copyright © 2024 Mary Webb Edlund.

All rights reserved. No part of this book may be reproduced, stored, or transmitted by any means—whether auditory, graphic, mechanical, or electronic—without written permission of both publisher and author, except in the case of brief excerpts used in critical articles and reviews. Unauthorized reproduction of any part of this work is illegal and is punishable by law.

ISBN: 979-8-89419-088-4 (sc)
ISBN: 979-8-89419-089-1 (hc)
ISBN: 979-8-89419-090-7 (e)

Because of the dynamic nature of the Internet, any web addresses or links contained in this book may have changed since publication and may no longer be valid. The views expressed in this work are solely those of the author and do not necessarily reflect the views of the publisher, and the publisher hereby disclaims any responsibility for them.

One Galleria Blvd., Suite 1900, Metairie, LA 70001
(504) 702-6708

*In memory of my parents, Lance and Elizabeth Webb,
who taught me that I am loved and never alone.*

Contents

Preface	*Wholeness in the Spirit*	ix
Chapter 1	*Know Yourself*	1
	God's Child	1
	The Heart and the Shell	7
	The Enneagram	8
	The Nine Types in the Enneagram	9
	The Myers-Briggs Inventory	13
Chapter 2	*Spirituality and Theology*	17
	Response to Spirit	18
	Examining Theology in the Light of New Science	19
	Awakening	21
Chapter 3	*The Soul and Wholeness*	31
	The Journey	31
	The Divided Life	33
	Finding the Way Home	40
Chapter 4	*Wholeness and Healing*	43
	Emotions	43
	Brokenness	48
	The Energetic System and Prayer	49
	Wholeness vs. Wellness	51
	Breath	53
	Stress	54
	Letting Go, Forgiveness	55
Chapter 5	*Growing Your Spirit*	59
	The Subjective/Internal Quadrant	65
	The Subjective External Quadrant	66
	The Objective /Physical Quadrant	67
	The Social (or Inter-Objective)	69

Chapter 6	*Stages of Spiritual Consciousness* 75
	First Chakra – The Root. 78
	Second Chakra – The Sacrum. 79
	Third Chakra – The Solar Plexus 81
	Fourth Chakra – The Heart 82
	Fifth Chakra – The Throat. 85
	Sixth Chakra – The Mind. 87
	Seventh Chakra – The Crown. 90
Chapter 7	*Living as God's Child*. 93
	Set Afire in Faith. 93
	Prayer as Energy 99
	Understand Your Gifts 100
	Examine Your Circumstances in the Light of Your Gifts. 102
	Live as God's Child. 103

About the Author 109
Resources 111
Bibliography 113
Endnotes. 115

PREFACE

Wholeness in the Spirit

When I was in my 30s, I discovered the concept of wholeness in the purpose statement for my women's group at church ("...to become whole persons through Jesus Christ."). It seemed to be an amorphous term—unclear, but important. Because of the pull of that word, I began to write poetry in my journal, and that started an amazing spiritual journey of growing toward wholeness. When I wrote "Work of the Spirit," I was inviting God's Spirit to come, live and work in me. The miracle was that was all that was needed. The discoveries I've made since then are the source of this book. I believe wholeness is the secret to a meaningful life – a life lived in the awareness of Spirit's presence.

Work of the Spirit

(John 15:26-27)

Deeper than knowledge
Now a part of who I am
Spirit, speak to me.

Beneath my conscious willing
Delve into secret regions
Where words are yet unformed.

God, who formed my soul,
Come there to live, to kindle life.
Create in me your fire.

Then shall I express
In who I am and shall become
Your reflection gift.

Spirit, love through me.
Escape my timid heart's control
To love creatively.

In these pages, I examine two elements that help forge our lives and make us who we are: Spirit, an invisible presence, and Wholeness, a state of being. Every one of us possesses these two elements, but most of us either ignore them or count them beyond our power to grasp. They're too invisible. We can't measure them. The irony is that we are each born with these two essential gifts and carry them with us throughout our lives. They make us who we are.

The *Spirit* that we are born with is the source of our life and our connection with the Eternal. In this context, I spell the word *Spirit* a capital S, in reference to its life-force connection with God. Christians, coming from the Judeao-Christian tradition, refer to it as the Holy Spirit. All of us have this life-giving, elemental breath within us. God created each one of us, and breathes through us every moment. The soul is not the Spirit but a receptacle for the Spirit.

The word *Spirit* has its roots in many ancient languages, and in most of them it has a complex meaning. It not only implies wind, but also implies breath and life-force: in Hebrew, it's *Ruach*; in Sanskrit, it's *Prana*: in Greek, it's *Pneuma*. The English word *Spirit* has lost the implied connection with breath, perhaps due to the Age of Enlightenment, where rationality and reason dominated Spirit, so that inspiration and creativity remained simply a quirk of life. In the Western world, the dominance of rationality categorized Spirit as too mystical to measure, so why bother. Now, in the 21st Century, we are searching for Spirit as the missing link. Without it, we understand that we wouldn't even be alive. Our connection with the Eternal through our Spirit is our clearest path to understand our uniqueness, our distinct spiritual DNA and emotional blueprint. That blueprint also defines our *Wholeness*. Without this Spirit connection, we cannot be all that we were created to be.

When we were newly born, we were as close to being a whole person as we will ever be. We were babes resting in the arms of the Creator – trusting, willing to ask for what we needed, full of hope and love, glad to be who we were and offering ourselves unashamedly. Even if our bodies were not born perfect, or if our minds could not function at the highest levels of intelligence, we were whole because we were immersed in the Love that created us, living in harmony with God at all levels: heart, mind and soul. With the Spirit breathing in us and sensing our completeness in

God's love and our connection with all of life, we were concrete expressions of God's miracle of life.

After we were born, the Breath of Life made its home in our bodies, and our autonomic nervous systems continued our breathing without our having to worry about it. Our hearts pumped, our digestive organs functioned, our senses connected to our minds for interpretation, and we began to live life in search of autonomy: "I'm in charge of my life, and I can manage it by myself." Wishful thinking. We learned that we couldn't do it all by ourselves. Our parents became our managers, our teachers, and our nurturers. We were dependent, but oh, how we wanted to be independent, to grow up and be our own bosses. Thus, from the beginning, we showed our parents our more demanding natures, crying when we didn't get our way.

All through childhood, this conflict manifested as we learned what we could be in charge of and what someone else would tell us to do. In this struggle, by the age of 8 or 9, we set arbitrary boundaries between ourselves, others and God, and we began to lose our essence, the wholeness that had given us such peace as infants. We began to wonder whom we could trust, who or what could give us all we needed to be happy. We began to be self-conscious, trying to please those who would judge us, trying to be someone they wanted us to be. Who we really were was shoved into the background of our lives, and we sought love from someone outside us. Eventually, we didn't remember who we really were. But it's still in there inside us – that knowledge, that congruence with God's Spirit that will bring us back to wholeness – and we can learn how to open up to it.

Although this is not a book of psychology, the struggles involved in growing up shape our lives, our self-concept, and our relationship with Spirit. Lucky are the children whose primary nurturers sought to bring out the highest good in their proteges and not just what they thought was best. Our struggle to grow up teaches us what we think about ourselves and how to successfully approach life's decisions. Eventually, we do need to separate ourselves from our parents and be effective in dealing with life's challenges. But how much of our true selves have we lost, especially when, all along, the Spirit presence is within us, calling us to be authentically who we are, to learn to love ourselves, others and God – in other words, to be whole?

When I was a teenager, I deeply wanted to become an "autonomous" person. I wanted to be able to take care of myself, to be responsible for my actions, and to lose my dependence on my parents or anyone. I thought that dependence was the worst of weaknesses for an adult, so I questioned why I should want to depend on God for anything. Dependence became a theological dilemma for me, since my upbringing as a Methodist preacher's kid urged me to depend completely on God. I struggled with my faith in those years because of my definition of autonomy. What I had to learn was that the Spirit that lives in me is the source of my life and my autonomy. Through the Spirit, God is a part of who I am, and not some external force making me do something. With God as part of me, I can be more autonomous, not less. I began a life-long quest for Spirit. What did it mean? How was spirituality different from theology?

I decided I wanted to be whole more than autonomous. I knew my broken places, and I wanted to know how to heal them. But what did wholeness mean? It was this journey that inspired my calling to the ministry of healing and wholeness, which I could barely define at the time; and yet, I was convinced of its connection to health and happiness.

I discovered I truly was God's child, and that Spirit was my teacher. Throughout this book, I will offer other poems that I have written as I listened to the Spirit within me. They have been messages of Life for me, and I hope they will strike a chord with you as well.

God's Child

God comes to me where I am…
God enters into my thinking and my believing
To give me life
To guide my spirit
to a new level of comfort
courage
compassion.
I am shaped for God's good pleasure.
And it is *my* pleasure
to be a part of God's creation
Here for God's purpose
God's future
God's service.

To meet God face to face
Calms all striving, fades all fear,
Fills my empty spaces
With who I really am.
God-created
God's beloved Child

CHAPTER 1

Know Yourself

How great is the love the Father has lavished on us, that we should be called children of God! And that is what we are!

1 John 3:1 NIV

Have you noticed that at one level or another, you are always your parents' child? Your parents may recognize that you have grown up and have a certain level of maturity, but in their hearts, they see you as their child – the little one they gave birth to, nurtured, taught and guided, worried over, disciplined, and most of all, loved. Not all parents have given an equal amount of these, but in their own way, they did feel a connection with you that will last all your life. Even after they've gone, their imprint is strong, and you find yourself doing things just as they did, without even thinking about it. The problem with human parents is that they have their own flaws and immaturities that keep them from seeing you as the person you were created to be. These flaws can be passed on without conscious choice to break the patterns.

God's Child

You are first and foremost God's child, in the keeping of those earthly parents. God has a connection with you in a way that your earthly parents could never have. God can see into your heart and soul and spirit, and can speak to you and lead you to do things that are uniquely yours to do.

The problem becomes recognizing and listening to that Spirit of God within you.

At one time or another, even as a child, you may have wondered, "Why am I the only one who knows what's going on in my head?" "Why do I feel so separate?"

When I was four, I began to experience these feelings, and I even asked my daddy why am I who I am, and I said to him tearfully, "You don't really know who I am from the inside, do you?"

God's Own Dear Child

My own dear child,
You are my inheritance
— child of my heart
— seed of my hope
— fruit of my love
And upon your heart I write my promise
Joy — Hope — Love
to shine in you
My stars dance upon your heart.
reflect in your eyes
sing your special song
You are my gift
with imprint so clear
no one can mistake
from whom you came
for whom you live
My own dear child
My precious life in flesh
Draw near your heart
That my life may live in you

That was a strange question for a little girl, but I had just awakened from a dream about that very thing. I dreamed that I was an experiment. All the people in heaven were watching me and how I reacted to situations and lived my life. They were trying to understand me, coach me for a good life. I dreamed they were making a movie of me so that they could study it. Probably some psychologist could attribute the dream to my being a preacher's kid, on display for the congregation, and trying to please everyone. At four years old? But beyond that, I knew I was not really alone, and my dream was a kind of twisted proof of it to my little self.

My father assured me that I wasn't being recorded by the angels in heaven, but I kept an innate belief that I wasn't alone. I was being guided. That spiritual awareness was more important to me than trying to please people, even though I have done my share of that. My awareness of the "company of angels" who loved me and watched over me stayed with me in growing up, because of that very real dream so early in my life. None of us is alone. We may be set apart to do a specific work, but we are a part of all God's creation. And in it, we are each very specially loved. If I am, certainly you are too!

Nothing we do goes without consequence, because we were put here on this earth with unique gifts (our essence) to be the person that God created us to be. What we do with those gifts is up to us. The sadness is that many of us never understand how important we are, and we go around discrediting ourselves, feeling useless or unloved, ready to give up when times get tough.

I Do Not Go Alone

Naked innocence
– no showy baubles, silken scarves –
Bare trust
– vulnerable to light and heat – pain or affliction
Standing still before God
– a creation not alone.
That is how God sees me.
That is how God loves me.
When I am sent
I do not go alone.
A presence fills my heart
Power overwhelms my soul.
Jesus enters
Leads me through the brambles of my confusion
to the sandy shores of peace,
to life made full
And I do not go alone.

The deeper understanding of "Child of God" came to me in my mid-twenties, as I was dealing with fears for a pregnancy and reading some comforting books. I put down John Powell's book, **Fully Human, Fully Alive**, and I began to cry. God really did love me! I felt it in my heart. My life really did have a purpose, and I really did have a family that loved me and was making this journey with me. I would be all right.

Maybe because my name is Mary I am drawn to Jesus' mother, Mary, and her response to God in her Magnificat (Luke 1:26-38). She truly was chosen, but we are each chosen for something we might think is impossible. I knew I was chosen, too. My response had to be: *"How can this be, Lord? You choose ME?—but for what?"*

The Possibility

God sees the possibility
And chooses the impossible.
When I see the impossibility
I choose only the possible.
But GOD looked at Mary
saw the promise
in a youthful, faithful heart
open to God's blessing,
And God said,
"You will be my son's mother."
How can this be?
Has God has rightly chosen?
Can she trust in none other than God?
"Here I am," she replies.
"Let it be with me according to your word."
The impossible is possible with God?
So let it be with me, dear Lord!

The Heart and the Shell

But God can't use me until I can open myself up to Spirit. Often the most difficult task in or lives is being open to God because we have so many layers of sadness, cover-up, insecurity to get through before we can even see who we really are as God sees us.

These layers could be called our "shell." That wall we build around our hearts to cover up the pain, the accusation, the rejection has, little by little, become a massive fortress. Not wanting to let anyone in, we keep our true selves as hidden away as possible. False personality, consisting of our egocentric defenses, develops as we strive to *survive* in the physical world, where trust is not always a reality. It develops in order to protect and defend our *essence* from injury in the material world.[1]

Our ego-created boundaries keep us from living in attunement with the environment and others. These boundaries become defenses for our threatened essence, separating us from this essential connection with Spirit. We function as automatons, choosing our behavior on the basis of habit – safety in the familiar. We allow no room for creative thought or action as we retreat from any new possibility. When our shell is thick enough, we really are automatons, and probably quite incomplete.

When I think of the beauty and abundance of God's grace raining down on us every moment of our lives, I see this shell around our heart as an umbrella, a shield that protects us from anything that might impact our lives. The shield blocks out the good and the bad, but mostly the good, because there is more of it than bad. We are protecting ourselves from everything, even God. And what a loss that is. The umbrella is preventing the cleansing, renewing rain of God's grace that will show us who we really are and give us wisdom and strength to deal with life's problems. The umbrella stops that connection, even though we still breathe in and out, and our autonomic nervous system still functions. We are completely disconnected, incongruent in mind, body and spirit, living a life separate from the Spirit that makes us whole.

The spiritual path is one of openness, of hope and acceptance, trusting that there is more to life than what we can see or even comprehend. It is a path that is shared with our Creator each moment, each step, at each new turn and each new horizon. To walk this life in the awareness of our Spirit connection is an expression of wholeness that can only bring health, harmony and joy in living, even in desperate circumstances.

Our awareness must be expanded to understand who we are from the inside out – why we respond to others the way we do, why we make the choices we do, why we get hurt over certain things that don't make any difference to someone else. God made us each unique, and from our hardened-shell point of view, it is hard to understand our uniqueness without putting ourselves down. We need to understand the essence of ourselves so that we can deal more authentically with others.

The Enneagram

More basic to our spiritual self-understanding is an awareness of our shell and the worldview that we have imposed upon ourselves. The ancient system of the Enneagram can take us into a deeper awareness of the habits and preoccupations that keep us from functioning as whole persons. The name, "Enneagram" comes from the Greek *ennea*, meaning "nine," and *grammos*, meaning "points." From the Christian monks of 399 A.D. and Sufi mystics, the system has been adapted and used by Franciscans, medieval Islamic Sufi, and more recently the Jesuits. In 1971, the Jesuits combined psychology, spirituality and theology in a holistic model to use it in its present form. This inventory of spiritual types has been recently expanded for use in the psychological evaluation of personality. If you have the opportunity to take and study the inventory, discovering more intimately who you are and what motivates you, your Spirit connection will deepen. Using the Enneagram, you will do inner work for self-knowledge and learn to see yourself in the light of God's unconditional love.

The nine points on this Enneagram star suggest that there are nine major aspects of essential being, and that each one approaches life in a slightly different way. Each has light and darkness, harmful traits and redeeming traits. The Enneagram measures our most dominant traits as they were in our 20s and 30s, when we were young and least self-aware. As we grow older, the process of maturity softens the lines that make us one type or another, and hopefully, we come to a place where we are able to take on more redeeming qualities from all the types. An enneagram analysis of Jesus, done by Richard Rohr, notes that Jesus has traits of all the types.[2] When we can objectively become aware of why we do the things we do, we see ourselves more as God sees us.

The Nine Types in the Enneagram[3]

The Enneagram is a dynamic movement. We all have the potential to be any of the nine types, although we will identify most strongly with one type. The interconnecting lines can suggest to us the versatility of movement between types, where we go when we are under stress, what feeds us when we are at ease.

This chart can help you see how the different Types approach life. Each type has its usefulness in this world, so there is no "good" or "bad" type. For instance, **Type 8**, the Protector, has experienced injustice in his/her life, and wants to correct it with strength. This type uses a strong personality to take over when someone needs rescue and stands up for a cause. Sometimes classified as a "Leader," this is not the mild-mannered, thoughtful person who can heal situations, but instead relies on the might makes right philosophy.

Type 9, the Mediator, has also been called the "Sloth." This is simply a description of one's ability to observe and not act. Their self-restraint makes them good mediators. Lack of impetuousness can help when opposing views are presented.

The primary trait of a **Type 1** personality is their need to be right, to make the right choice, to do the right thing. Rohr calls it "The Perfectionist." This conscientiousness is admirable except when it gets in the way of making a decision or becomes judgmental to those folks who do not have such a built-in need for correctness. Vexation is a nice way of saying how they feel when others do not go along with them.

A **Type 2** person, the Giver, makes a good caregiver, because she notices what people need and makes a special effort to give it to them. Two problems in this type may appear: If the person being served doesn't appreciate the service, then the Giver becomes resentful; or the Giver may fail to ask for help for herself when she really needs it.

The **Type 3**, Performer, works to make a good impression in all that he does. As a child, it really mattered to be first in the class, or best in the test. The child craves the special attention he received for those feats. A Type 3 personality can juggle many projects and come out looking good. Self-image is their most important concern. Of course, failures can be devastating.

Type 4, the Romantic/Artist, is a melancholy type, who feels deeply and can be influenced by events to take on their drama. They often dress in black or dramatic colors. They want to be unique, different, and authentic. They require special care from their loved ones.

The Nine Types in the Enneagram

Type	Descriptor	Temptation	Self-Image	Avoidance
1	Perfectionist	Perfection	I am right	Vexation
2	Giver	Helping Others	I help	Suppressing Neediness
3	Performer	Efficiency	I am successful	Failure
4	Romantic	Authenticity	I am different	Ordinariness
5	Observer	Knowledge	I see through	Emptiness
6	Loyal Skeptic	Security	I do my duty	Inappropriate Behavior
7	Epicure	Idealism	I am happy	Pain
8	Protector	Justice	I am strong	Weakness
9	Mediator	Self-deprecation	I am content	Conflict

Type 5, The Observer uses his analytic mind to dissect and study everything. They make good scientists. Generally, persons of this type are not extroverts, but they do appreciate the company of others like them and gravitate toward social groups of their peers.

Type 6, the Loyal Sceptic, is bound to duty. They need security in their lives, and if it is lacking, they will go to extremes to find it – even joining militaristic groups in which to place their loyalty. Things must be done in traditional ways, with no room for change.

Type 7, is the Epicure, sometimes called "Glutton." This person likes to try just about everything – taking risks, having adventures. Type 7 is a generalist who looks at everything as something interesting, but not with intent of going deeper.

When I first took the Enneagram inventory in 1994, I couldn't accept Type 7 as my type. I was offended by that classification, because it implied that as a generalist, I was shallow. A Type 7 is also an idealist, seeing what could be more than what is. The dark side of the Type 7 is the need to avoid pain. It was actually painful to admit that I was so much of what I called a "ditz." This is typical of a person's reaction to discovering her type. We like to deny what is most real in ourselves. I thought that Type 7 may be a part of my personality, but not my guiding type. **For everyone, the type that you don't want to be is usually your type.**

Type 8 is the Protector, who leads with authority and determination, wanting to get justice for the underdog because of his own experiences of injustice. It is a forceful person more than a gentle person. Each type has its own redeeming qualities as well as its needs for avoidance (such as "pain" for a Type 7), thus making some good and some not-so-good choices to deal with life's challenges.

As we become more aware of how we make our choices in life, we can learn how to open our shells, mature to a more authentic self, and learn to deal with the not-so-good responses that our shell has made automatic with us.

This is a simplified introduction. The study of your type on the Enneagram requires leadership, trust, study and discussion, and it is best made in a circle of friends of different types. Several excellent resources listed in the resource pages at the end of the book can help you delve into your personality using this method. I highly recommend the experiential test form found in **The Essential Enneagram, The Definitive Personality Test and Self-Discovery Guide**, written by David Daniels, M.D., and Virginia Price, Ph.D. Unlike other inventories theirs is not a questionnaire, but a system of reading about each type and classifying oneself inductively. Academic understanding can be gained by reading works of Helen Palmer on the Enneagram, and Richard Rohr and Andreas Ebert as an in-depth Spirit-centered model.

Life's journey will never be easy or even painless. It is in these difficult moments that we need the anchor of Spirit within that reassures us of our worth and is our wholeness. Yes, we must go through the chaos of change, the disappointments of failure, and the grief of loss, but how we come through on the other end depends on our anchor. If our only anchor is self-hatred and condemnation, then we are lost and without hope.

The key word in our spiritual quest is *awareness*. Am I aware that I am more than I ever could comprehend? Am I aware that I am spiritually connected with all of life, that I am not alone, and that I never will be? Proof of God is not the awareness I need. Proof is head stuff and will only lead to discouragement and confusion. We do need to process the relationship through our minds, however. We were the given the gift of rationality to integrate our mind with our Spirit. Writing out our thoughts is often helpful. Reading spiritual writings can open us to new understanding. Meditating in quiet solitude can bring amazing revelation. What we must let go is fear of new understanding, so that Spirit can truly work within us.

The Myers-Briggs Inventory

Psychological inventories can help us discover ways our personality can naturally connect with Spirit. The Myers-Briggs Inventory of personality type is available in many forms online, and you may search for them on the Internet with the key words, *Myers Briggs*. The shortened inventory forms are not as accurate as the psychologist-administered MBTI® but they can begin to point you in the direction to understand your spiritual tendencies. The analysis is based on four type indicator scales:

- I/E: Introvert/Extravert (how we get our energy)
- S/I: Sensing/Intuition (how we take in information)
- T/F: Thinking/Feeling (how we make decisions and come to judgments)
- J/P: Judging/Perceiving (how we relate to the external world—orderly or open-ended).
- Each person scores somewhere along each of these scales, where they discover, ISTJ, INTJ, etc.)

In their book, **Prayer and Temperament,** Chester P. Michael and Marie C. Norrisey have made an analysis of the spiritual temperament of the 16 possible combinations. They show how each person will approach the Spirit in his or her own way.[4] The combination of two indicators provides a spiritual type; for instance, the NF of an E<u>NF</u>P, I<u>NF</u>P, E<u>NF</u>J and I<u>NF</u>J shows dominant *I<u>N</u>tuitive* and auxiliary *<u>F</u>eeling* tendencies, and is less likely to <u>S</u>ense or <u>T</u>hink about Spirit. Instead, one intuits a personal and deep spiritual relationship without analyzing them. These personalities most easily adapt to St. Augustine's prayer form, as his personality type uses *Intuition* and *Feeling* to interpret one's personal situation. People with other characteristics on the Myers-Briggs score will connect with the Spirit in differently.

Michael and Norrisey identify three other combinations: SP, SJ, and NT, which resemble the spiritual traits of other saints: SP for the Franciscan type of St. Francis of Assisi, SJ for the Ignatian type of St. Ignatius of Loyola, and NT for the Thomistic type of Thomas Aquinas.

The Franciscan *Sensing/Perceiving* (SP) personality connects with Spirit by communing with Nature and Creation in spontaneous prayer and acts of mercy; the Ignatian *Sensing/Judging* personality finds order in the practice of *Lectio Divina*, an organized formula for daily meditation; the Thomistic *Intuitive/Thinking* personality is more comfortable with a deep, contemplative, mystical union with God.[5] As we recognize our spiritual nature, we can more naturally express our uniqueness in our relationship with God. Understand that we can also find connection in the spiritual expressions of other types that go beyond our natural inclinations. This awareness can help us grow and perhaps broaden how we approach our relationship with Spirit.

An open awareness to Spirit's companionship will change your journey – *alone* but not lonely, *curious* but not obsessed, *responsive* more than reactive. Friend or foe or stranger will look different to you. You can be free to forgive and to love because you see each one with this Spirit's eye. Each one has a blessing to offer. This is the outlook of wholeness, and it is different indeed!

Practice and Ideas to Ponder

1. How does it make you feel to know that there is a presence within you that knows you better than you know yourself? Are you afraid or comforted? Write a letter to that presence to express how you feel.

2. What experiences in your life have made you feel you are not alone, that there is a presence of love within that is your constant companion? If you have no experience with this, spend some time in quiet meditation on the phrase, "I am loved."

3. Meditating on the illustration of the heart and shell, list specific instances of your life when you acted out of the shell, then specific instances when you acted from your heart.

4. When circumstances have been defeating, and you are feeling anxious or depressed, what is the most natural way for you to reach out for Spirit?

5. How can you relate to Spirit with your mind and not just your heart?

CHAPTER 2

Spirituality and Theology

But the wisdom that comes from heaven is first of all pure; then peace-loving, considerate, submissive, full of mercy and good fruit, impartial and sincere.

James 3:17-18 NIV

I had never used the term "spirituality" to describe a person until I had spent time working with the Little Sisters of the Poor, a Catholic religious order. One of the sisters had said to me, "Don't you just love Jeanne Jugan's spirituality? (She was the founder of their order.) I had to pause to respond. I didn't really understand the word *spirituality*. The nun helped me by saying, "You know, how Jeanne Jugan lived her life for the poor, begged for food for them, housed them." Aha! I thought, she means how her faith influenced her actions – her spirituality! I hadn't realized that spirituality implied actions and a relationship with God, not just belief.

At the end of my first theology course in seminary, I felt compelled to ask my professor how spirituality relates to theology. This had become my burning question.

The seminary professor scoffed at my question, as though theology and spirituality didn't relate at all. He didn't address my question any further, except to point out that spirituality is experiential, and theology is rational (and never the twain shall meet?). I felt put down, because, of course, we do connect them as we formulate a faith.

Response to Spirit

If you experience Spirit, you also respond in some way to it. What the Spirit reveals is interpreted by action and rationality: thinking about it, valuing it, doing something about it. Our response might be to make the decision to believe in it, which is theology, the study of God. So in this case, the experience comes first, then the analysis. It could start from the other side, though, with an intellectual longing to *know*, an approach that would be natural to a Type 5 on the Enneagram.

Analysis requires data, and experience is one form of data. In the Wesleyan tradition, we look at experience, reason, tradition and scripture to help us understand our faith. So the experience of Spirit can precede its analysis. To put it in concrete terms, once I have experienced the presence of Spirit and know what it does for and in me, I can begin to formulate what I believe about it, or "theologize." Some theologians theologize without experience, working only from ideas. This theology, in my mind, is weak because it is thirdhand and never personal.

This world has as many theologies as there are people, only most people aren't aware that they are theologians. Group spirituality has been the source of many religions in the world, and even within a religion we divide into so many sects, so many denominations, and even cults. In an effort to codify their theologies, groups formulate a religion to set themselves apart or make them feel special or wiser.

For example, the Hebrews wrote down their stories in their scriptures about God's activity in their lives and how God brought them together as a chosen people. They interpreted Spirit's presence among them as the guiding force that allowed them to prosper and survive in spite of hardships. They noted an intense personal presence of Spirit in their prophets who, despite personal imperfections, were able to "hear God's voice" clearer than others. Their religion was based on the experience of these special people, whose influence created the theology of a personal God. Their journey of life was a spiritual journey.

Most of our theologizing is a result of where we are in our process of human development. I will go into more detail on this in a later chapter, but for now, let us look at the tribal mentality that existed in the people of early Mesopotamia. They attributed the powers of fertility, love, hunting and warfare to gods who know how to give us those powers. Even today, we pray to the "god" in charge of what we want—money or power. In this primitive mind, the gods are to be manipulated rather than related to, for our prayers are only for personal gain. When that is the case, God is outside us, not within us.

In today's world, an abundance of choice is available in the theological interpretation of our experiences, and modern people are finding that new scientific information on the energy of matter opens up even more possibilities. Energy is an expression of Spirit, but only now are we beginning to understand how. So when these discoveries come in conflict with our religious beliefs, we find ourselves wondering if we can throw out the old (which still has much value for us) for the new (which is not entirely formed), or whether we should stubbornly cling to obsolete belief just to stay in our comfort zone, obstinately implying that we are the only ones who know the Truth.

Examining Theology in the Light of New Science

This choice was mine when I took an energy healing course at the local hospital. I knew intuitively that what I was feeling in my hands was Spirit's energy flowing between me and my patient. I didn't fully understand how it worked, but I knew that my energy worked on the energy levels of the patient, and that it made a difference in their healing. As a Christian, I saw how this could be a tiny step toward understanding the healing that Jesus did so naturally. I became spiritually aware of my own powers and of another person's need. Fundamentalist Christians would condemn me for using supernatural powers to heal as Jesus healed. My experience called me to examine the basis for my faith in healing and to see that this did not negate my faith, but instead increased it. I felt my spiritual connection with God more deeply and saw the results of this collaboration in the improved condition of those I worked on. I was careful to center myself in Spirit for this collaboration to be most effective.

Thus, my theology expanded. I understood more clearly that I am an instrument of God in all I do on earth. I came to believe that I had the potential to touch with God's love in everything I said or did, and so

I took my role as God's ambassador more seriously I could begin to see myself as a healer! This thought is very biblical, but with a closed mind, it would not be recognized. My study groups often shook their heads at Jesus' admonition to his disciples: "I tell you the truth, anyone who has faith in me will do what I have been doing. He will *do even greater things than these*, because I am going to the Father.[6] They couldn't imagine that! Just like Jesus' disciples, we say, "How can that be?" And again, in the book of Matthew: "When the disciples heard this, they were greatly astonished and asked, 'Who then can be saved?' Jesus looked at them and said, 'With man this is impossible, but with God all things are possible.' (Matt 19:25-28)

Jesus was called "The Christ." Christ is not his last name. Christ reflects God. Christ can be described as a form of Spirit that was so strong in Jesus that he could do more than anyone thought possible through acts of love. Jesus was talking about the Christ Spirit that can live in each one of us as we develop an awakened awareness of how we are connected to God's love.

I believe we have barely touched on the power that is within us because of the presence of the Spirit. We are living in an age of new awareness and understanding because of scientific breakthroughs in quantum theory with all those quarks and sparks that are controlled by our thoughts and our energy (Spirit)! Did you know, for instance, that particles change their movement when they are being observed? Scientific observation during experiments actually changes the results of the experiment. To many, this implies that our thoughts have energy to influence matter at its tiniest. Now is the time for this awareness to grow and develop. It will take an openness to Spirit and the discipline of theology cultured in our experience as well as tradition, reason and scripture for us to understand how truly inter-connected we all are through this energy.

At the Hesychia Spiritual Direction Training retreat in Tucson, Arizona, our group was exposed to class members and lectures from the major religions of the world. We sought to discover our similarities beyond our differences. The morning of the presentation on Buddhism, my synchronistic devotional reading was from Jesus' prayer: "I have given them the glory that you gave me, that they may be one as we are one: I in them and you in me. May they be brought to complete unity to let the world know that you sent me and have loved them even as you have loved me." [7]

Awakening

Jesus was speaking beyond his time, for his disciples could have never understood the true unity of our creation through our energy fields. That reading brought me an enormous epiphany that was not just by reason, but by intuition—illumination.

In my journal that day, I wrote, "In the new physics of energetics, we learn that our energy field is connected to every other energy field through our vortexes. In that sense, we are literally connected one to the other, all together!

"The psychic connection that our religion has frowned upon is a natural phenomenon for anyone who opens (empties) oneself enough to 'see' it."

Koinonia

Love is all around us,
In every song that sings,
In every breath life brings.

Community, where love is found
Becomes a special feeling
To open hearts revealing
A visible affirmation
Of God's love and confirmation
In every voice spoken,
In every bread that's broken.

We now can love each other
Because he first loved us,
Because we, too, are precious,
Each one to him unique,
Each strong where we were weak.

I'll praise my God each day until
Each one can feel his love
Each knows the meaning of
Christ's love in common unity
Where God's grace can touch
though me.

Any of us can come to such new awareness as we open to the additional spiritual dimensions of who we are, as Gautama Buddha did. He became "the awakened one," after sitting under a tree in contemplation for many days. He learned compassion for the poor and hungry, and he recognized his connectedness to all of humanity. A Buddha is called "The Awakened One." In that sense, when we allow ourselves this new awareness, we too are awakened ones, awake to the oneness of all life, as Jesus was. Interestingly, Buddha's awakening did not include the existence of God or even Spirit, but it didn't dis-include it.

Just as there are those who see the body of our unity as a vast net with a unique jewel at each juncture of the netting, we are all connected. The jewels reflect each other perfectly in balance, a metaphor for how much we are loved and connected in "Spirit." And to me, as a Christian, it implies the existence of God who has created us and loves us and lives in us.

Here I have theologized from an intuitive spiritual awakening. Let us not belittle our awakenings, even when they stretch our standard theology. Who knows what information is truly "right" and "wrong?" Theologians try to prove they know it, and we come out with many lines of what is "True;" but honestly, God only knows it. I believe God has created us to learn from these moments of insight by using our reason to test it against what we know in our hearts and minds.

Radical Dependency

I Cor. 12:12-27

That we might be one...
share courage
suffer
rejoice
find God
in community...
Radical dependency, God asks.

But in fear of losing identity
we shy away.
What more to lose than God
As we separate from the 'Body?'

Christ calls us back
Unites these separate selves
So fragile and so torn
Christ becomes the thread
Weaves the fragments into a vibrant whole
For beauty, strength and service.

Radical dependency,
God called it.

As to the Truth, Jesus said, "I am the Way, the Truth and the Life." Not just that what he said was the Truth, he said HE was the Truth. His life was true to his connection with God, a life that all of us can have when we follow and believe in him. We are called to live in the Truth.

Infinitely More

*God's power, working in us, can do infinitely
more than we can ask or imagine.*

Ephesians 3:14-21

Infinitely more...
More than I could ask
More than I could imagine.
God is power in me,
wonderfully and fearfully at work
to weave love into my heart.

I search to see within
The knots, the twists, the crossings
God carefully traces there...

My stories are God's
where strands of truth appear
where they intertwine in loving ways
to create a masterpiece.

To acknowledge each and every part --
past and present,
I, too, weave toward God's future.
Your love, O God, is intricately woven
in my spirit.
You fill my heart to overflowing.

I cannot count the paths,
Like grains of sand they have no number...
Infinity's boundaries stretch out before me.

I am infinitely more
with infinitely more to share.

Religions codify their beliefs so that people are not out there proclaiming that, by God's revelation, they are now qualified to lead people down paths of their own supremacy or equality with God. For those distortions and other reasons, religious leaders are frightened of independent theologians. It is truly frightening when we see the results of extremism in religious conflict and even wars. We need a measuring stick to see what is truly good. Christian theologians lift up Jesus and his life and teaching as that measuring stick. With Jesus as our anchor, we know we can't go off too far in the wrong direction. Each religion does have its own measuring stick, such as scripture, writings, and religious law.

When you consider the theological struggles between the early Christians and the Gnostics, the fear was that if Jesus was only wholly Divine, with no humanity in him, he didn't really experience our sufferings. Gnosticism pointed Christianity in a completely different direction, so the Christians developed creeds that emphasized that Jesus was wholly human *and* wholly Divine. If you don't believe that, you probably don't consider yourself a Christian, because Jesus' humanity is what makes him so inviting to follow.

But whatever path you are on, you are still a part of that vast net of diamonds that connects us all. And by Creation's intent, we are to find that connection.

God is God

God is a mystery.
I push for limits – definition.
I argue logic.
But God is God.

God, you are a mystery.
Tell me who you are!
I've felt your love
known your comfort
felt your presence
known your power.

You've given me curiosity to seek truth
A mind to reason
An imagination to create
And Jesus to show the way
To save me from my own destruction.

God *is* God
And God asks gently,
"Who do *you* say that I am?"

Practice and Ideas to Ponder

1. What are three essentials you consider for your theology? Make a timeline of your life and trace the foundational steps of your theology in your maturing process. What has influenced your growth or your discouragement? What role has Spirit played?

2. What spiritual insights have you had that might not be approved by your religious leaders? How do you balance this cognitive dissonance with your community of faith?

3. How is it important for you to have a community of faith? Have you ever been tempted to just leave it all and go off on your own? What draws you back?

CHAPTER 3

The Soul and Wholeness

> *When I came to the spring today, I said, 'O LORD, God of my master Abraham, if you will, please grant success to the journey on which I have come.*
>
> Gen 24:42-43 NIV

The Journey

Our life journey is a mysterious process. My sister, Jeanne, calls it "The Invisible Trail," meaning we never really know where we're going until we get there. She tells us, "I have been looking back and seeing that I have been following an INVISIBLE TRAIL that has been laid out for me. This trail is invisible to me for the future, but open for me to see when I look back.[8] Understanding is in hindsight, not in foresight. Life holds too many surprises. Our losses leave us dangling on the edge of hopelessness. Our triumphs lead us to believe we are invincible. Our joys leave us vulnerable to the reversal of fortune. We can become off-balance in the blink of an eye. We think we have it all, and then we have nothing. It is hard to live in the mystery of the journey if we don't travel in the companionship of Spirit, where trust and dependency keep us on track.

One popular way to look at our life journey is to compare it to a woven tapestry with a uniquely beautiful design on the front side, while on the back side is a jumble of threads knotted together. I like the idea of those knots. Those are the places where we stopped and changed direction -- colors or patterns where we disconnected and then connected to something else. Those knots are part of the process of life, but sometimes those knots are in places that needed to be worked out and shaped into a congruent design. If the choice we make is way off-base, then the thread been pulled too tightly, and the tension becomes too much for the design to support. We are all free to make choices, but the choices we make affect our well-being, our wholeness in relation to Spirit.

The Divided Life

Parker Palmer, in his book, **A Hidden Wholeness**, speaks of these poor choices as "the Divided Life." It's not so much about completion as it is about authenticity. When we decide to go ahead with something based on the needs of our fearful shell, we disconnect from our soul. Our decision negates who we really are. We help ourselves become someone our creator wouldn't recognize, or at least we couldn't recognize. Living the Divided Life leaves us blithely ignorant of what we're missing or completely frustrated with misunderstanding and brokenness. We're on a track toward literal self-destruction and oblivion, even though at the time we think we're playing it safe.

I am Light

I am light —
A dancing, radiating diamond in God's universe.
My light shines brightly, twinkles when I dance.
My light enlightens, enlivens, sets afire my soul
To dance God's melody.
But no, the darkness closes in
To hide me from God's light.
Is it fear? Is it Me?
Ah no, I'm fading, fading.
Drifting into darkness
Drifting into shame and sadness,
Drifting, drifting, smaller, darker,
To fit into this box of human understanding.

But God,
Come open that box.
Set me free
Ignite me in your love
So I may shine and dance again.
Breathe your breath of light and love into my heart.
Pulse my being with your love.
Turn me loose on your wings of joy
That I may forget myself, and remember only You!

Only your love, only your love. Amen.

The Soul and Wholeness

From Spirit's point of view, our fear of being who we really are extinguishes our inner light. We compartmentalize our choices and view our ethics as external codes of conduct, not as an expression of who we really are. Big business leaders who contributed to the financial ruin of the first decade of the 21st century are good examples of people who compartmentalized their ethics and let their greed and need of power overshadow their more compassionate selves. They deny the human consequences of their actions to serve only their bottom line. Athletes found guilty of steroid use are common in our society, compromising their integrity to fame and fortune. Politicians who only want the power of their position or party will say anything to discredit someone they disagree with, whether or not it is true or even makes sense. Inner darkness is all we see as we separate our living from the soul. We consciously separate our decision-making from the wisdom of the soul, and eventually we become fragmented and unauthentic, the opposite of whole.

Carolyn Myss, the medical intuitive, has described this divided life as taking on an archetype that is foreign to us.[9] One of the most common of these archetypes is "the Prostitute." We play the prostitute when we are willing to do something that goes against our values out of the fear of losing everything, In the fear for self-preservation, we prostitute ourselves, we give up what we value most.

The most common cause of this capitulation commonly comes down to money, sex or power. At a time in our country when the economy is unstable and jobs are hard to find, even a professional out of work could be tempted to gamble away all his resources – certainly dividing one's self from the authentic self. Prostitution comes in many forms other than the traditional sexual role, and none of us is exempt from it in one form or another. If the dividedness continues long enough, we lose ourselves in it.

When we live the Divided Life, favoring the external shell we have built around our hearts, we are living from our woundedness. If the shell is thick enough, we think our souls are safe—hidden away where we can forget them—and then lose them. But Spirit is always there, asking you to go deeper, calling you to dissolve that shell so you can heal your wounds in that loving presence that is waiting for you.

Weave Peace

God calls us to weave Peace
RECONCILE
Follow, Forgive, Love
Live, Discover,
Uncover Peace

TRUST
Spirit's presence
Spirit's provision
Where we hang our hope
To receive Peace.

ANTICIPATE
Wait expectantly
Being re-created
with mercy and loving kindness
To experience Peace.

JOYFUL
Spirit's power fills us
With love and deepest hope
To sing our song of promise
To rejoice in Peace.

DANCE
With our Creator.
Dip and flow, soar and float
Through trials and triumphs
Follow the Leader,
To weave Peace.

Often, our dividedness is more insidious: I don't want people to know who I really am, or they might not like me. I want people to think I'm a successful person instead of the failure I think I am.

This is self-talk. It starts with low self-esteem and comes out of our inner darkness. There is no light of love or self-acceptance in it. When I make myself believe that I'm worthless, this is the only way I can fool the world into liking me. Where is the Spirit and the love of God in this picture? It's hidden deep inside that shell, and completely disconnected.

Only by conscious choice can we stay whole even in the face of shattering reversals. We can choose the higher path to maintain our self-esteem and confidence. Wholeness is hard, because it is risky. What if things don't work out? What if I really am no good? What if I'm left destitute? We can imagine all the worst things when we don't allow the wisdom waiting in our soul to give us courage and determination. We can never feel worthy unless we feel loved, and the love of God is at the base of all our survival. If I've lost that connection, I really have lost my wholeness.

At our worst, we live as if we were truly helpless, blown from one crisis to another without the power or grace to survive. At best, the grace of Spirit as God's gift lives within us and rains through us every moment, making us more than we ever thought possible. Our authentic self is self, bathed in the grace of Spirit. It seems to be a paradox that with Spirit I am both greater than I could be and most authentically myself. H.A. Williams, in **Tensions**, says it best: "The more I discover within me the greater than me, the more I discover that the greater than me is authentically me."

Too Deep for Words

Likewise the Spirit helps us in our weakness, for we do not know how to pray as we ought, but the Spirit himself intercedes for us with sighs too deep for words.

Romans 8:26

Too deep for words
So deep I cannot fully understand
Where I am – What I need – What I will do
I feel so empty
(like a sock without a foot – shapeless, limp, cold)

Oh God, help!
I'm so muddy, muddled, muffled.
Can you hear?
My ears are deafened by *my* sighs
Of self-indulgent-pity-wallowing.
I can't hear – even me.

You can't help me, can you?
I won't let you, will I?
What will you do then, Lord?
Give me up?
Go help someone else?
Please don't leave!

Are you crying, Lord?
Are those sighs your sighs?
Are we together, even now?

You love me that much!

Burnout is a common symptom of the Divided Life. When I was a young woman doing communications in a chemical dependency treatment company, I realized that, even though I had no life experience with chemical dependency, I could have great empathy and was capable enough to write the stories about treatment. After some time, though, I found that I felt different from everyone I worked with, always under suspicion for not understanding chemical dependency from the dependent's perspective. I never felt good about my work or appreciated, and I became exhausted with the job. Was I just role-playing, being somebody I wasn't? I couldn't understand why my work exhausted me and didn't make me joyful or happy until I saw a counselor who diagnosed the burnout. I was doing something that could not allow me to be who I really was (innocent, naïve perhaps, but also empathic). I was leading the Divided Life. Now that may not seem too dramatic to you, but it was for me, and it required a job change, a risk in that job market. It also required some time alone, connecting to God through Spirit. The counselor asked me to spend 15 minutes each day in a rocking chair, repeating to myself, "I love you, Mary."

For complete recovery, the experience had to be followed by a wilderness time, a time of regrouping, letting go of what I thought I should be, and learning to trust in who I was, allowing Spirit to make me whole. Thomas Merton called it "the place of dark, of silence, of peace, the place of wrestling with the angel."[10]

The Divided Life is the wounded life that cries out for healing. We deny our pain or try to numb it with outside excesses – substance abuse, overwork, mindless media noise. Sometimes our psychic woundedness is as dangerous to our health as a physical illness and can even weaken our immunity to illness. This I learned in my energy healing training, and I hope that in the decades to come, more and more people will learn that their emotions are closely linked to their physical well-being. The result of the Divided Life can be life-threatening in more ways than we even acknowledge! In a later chapter, I will discuss these issues in more detail.

Finding the Way Home

Why do we pursue a spiritual path? To be healthy in mind, body and spirit, to be whole! We cannot be truly healthy when we are out of alignment. The secret to healing the Divided Life is inner integrity, or living an integrated life, where all the parts are processed—not just in the brain, but through the soul. The Spirit connection is basic to this integration, where the subconscious can speak as loudly as the conscious to our hearts.

The Möbius Strip[11]

Wholeness, the integrated life, is well-illustrated by the möbius strip, a circular strip with a front and back side that is twisted so that the front side moves seamlessly to the back. Bracelets in the möbius strip design are popular today, with scriptures or sayings printed on them that help remind us of the fluidity of life in Spirit. The möbius is a picture of actual wholeness, when you are so in touch with your soul that all you say and do comes from the foundation of who you are. What a reminder this is to live the seamless life, where what I practice and what I truly am are one.

The saying I would like to put on one of these bracelets is by Ralph Waldo Emerson: "What lies behind us and what lies before us are tiny matters compared to what lies within us." Wearing this around my arm, I could get my priorities straight. It's not what others think of me for past or future accomplishments. The important thing is being who God made me to be, so that I can appreciate others for who they really are. I would be reminded of the Spirit connection that will bring me home to understand who I really am.

Practice and Ideas to Ponder

1. Think about what hindsight wisdom you have gained in your life journey. How would you have changed things if you had known?

2. Sometimes we judge the tapestry of our lives as a mess more than a masterpiece. Spend some time meditating on how God sees your life and has worked in you to bring you through your mistakes to be a more whole person. Draw a picture of the back side of the tapestry.

3. As you look at your list of "shell" choices, recognize them as times you lived the Divided Life. What risks would you have had to take to live an integrated life with Spirit?

4. How do you love yourself? What are some practices or talismans you have that help you remember who you are and how you are loved?

5. Make a Möbius bracelet out of a piece of paper ½ inch by 8 inches long. Select a favorite quotation and write it out on the paper, continuing it on the back side. Twist the strip once, and then tape the ends together. Enjoy your own Möbius bracelet!

CHAPTER 4

Wholeness and Healing

May God himself, the God of peace, sanctify you through and through. May your whole spirit, soul and body be kept blameless at the coming of our Lord Jesus Christ. The one who calls you is faithful, and he will do it.

1 Thess 5:23-24 NIV

Emotions

Leading the undivided life doesn't rescue us from the emotional turmoil of life's challenges: health, family, job. Emotions are gifts to us, so that we can recognize what we are grieving for, what things are important to us, what we need to pay attention to. Emotions can help cleanse us and give us a clue to where our body/mind/spirit needs healing.

During a time when I was under much stress in my job, I found that I couldn't cry, even at a sappy movie! I steeled myself against tears so that I could just get through the challenges of work. I was "strong woman," and nothing was going to stop me. In the meantime, my back gave way, and I had to stay strong through much physical pain. I went to the doctor for my back, but what I was hiding from myself was that the back pain was my body reacting to the stress of not allowing myself to feel the pain and grief of my work.

To suppress emotion only aggravates the problem because we are not dealing with it. I wrote the poem, *Too Deep for Words* (from the last chapter), at such a time, when I felt disconnected from the Spirit. The act of writing my feelings led me to hear the Spirit whisper to me how much I am loved, and that I was not alone in my journey. Those times of comfort can only come when we can be honest about our feelings. Our closest companion in this life journey is the Divine, spoken to us through Spirit.

Tears are like Holy Water flowing down our cheeks, reminding us of the water of life that we have been given. They wash out the clogged passageways of our bodies, where old hurts and resentments fester. Be thankful for tears. They are a river flowing to Spirit because they help us to let go.

Tears are the easiest physical symptom to help us recognize that there is a problem in our life. Less physically obvious symptoms are fatigue, anger, fear, anxiety – but all are tied to emotions! In the first chapter, we talked about the importance of being self-aware. We're back to that place again that we can't ignore. *Know yourself,* and know why you are experiencing these emotions. Take the time to understand. Understanding requires thought and thought works to help us change.

Perfect Love Meets Fear Face to Face

Genesis 32:22 - 33:11

God's perfect love
Meets fear face to face
Welcomes it
Hears it
Loves it back
to trust.
Fear is a spirit
that leaps from inside
from the depth of the unknown
No solid comfort
No center to bring it to rest
Formless and free
it spreads infection
and darkens the world
around the soul.
God's wisdom casts an anchor
to hold fear fast
and nurture it back into the heart.
The cure, in loving gentleness
begins a new creation
where pulls and pushes
bring acceptance
birth a vision.
God, holding my fear
Offers it as a blessing
a loving touch
to teach me trust
and be made new.

Paying attention to our emotions is the beginning of wisdom. When we are self-aware, we can ask the right questions of ourselves or let the Spirit ask them. God will confront us at the level of emotions and use them to motivate a response and bring healing and hope. Because emotion is at the core of faith and love, it can bring us compassion, peace and self-esteem, which make a big difference in the choices we make in living healthy lives.

Our body/mind/spirit is one enormous interconnected system of life and health. When one part is weak, the other parts must put in extra energy to help that part get better. When I am angry, that anger is blocking me at an energetic level, resembling a dark splotch of infection hovering over my physical body. Our bodies can heal themselves with their own energy (Chi, Prana, Spirit), but only when we are honestly self-aware. We must consciously deal with our anger. When we are unaware of our emotion, we are living the Divided Life, and it can be physically dangerous.

Spirit can help us deal with our negative emotions. Fear is a result of the threat to the shell that we have wrapped around our heart in the Divided Life. Fear for self-preservation can happen in any life-threatening situation, and fear can be felt very well without the shell. The difference is, *with* the shell, we are on the defensive. *Without* the shell, Spirit can bring us to deal with the fear constructively. We can see the choice before us to find courage, based in the love that is within us. We will have confidence to seek the help we need or to do what has to be done. When we connect with the Spirit within, we can say, "I am not my fear. I am larger." The emotional freedom found in that statement has moved us from the small ego-self to the courageous spirit-filled self, or from the false shell to the heart itself.

Mary Webb Edlund

Brokenness

Life can deal out some bitter blows. We can succumb to their force, fall apart (either by being sick in body or sick in mind) and give up, shattered and sick at heart.

A little incident of minor tragedy gave me a concrete picture of what brokenness is like. After my mother died, I inherited her beautiful set of china. I treasured it because it was hers, and it would remind me of her every time I used it. When we moved into our new house, I put it on a windowed shelf in my cupboard where I would always see it. Early one morning, about six weeks after we moved in, we heard an enormous crash coming from the kitchen. Running to check it out, I found that the shelf had given way, and most of the plates and cups had fallen out of the cupboard and crashed against the countertop and the floor, shattering into a thousand pieces. At first I thought about how much money we didn't have to replace the set. But then I realized it wasn't the money I was grieving over; it was the loss of a very precious memory connection for me.

One of my favorite mugs has the Bible verse, "Thou art the Potter, I am the clay." To me, shattered pottery represents brokenness and loss in Spirit, and loss of hope. All the work of my mother's life seemed wrapped in those broken shards. I wondered how I could resurrect them in to new life. Then I remembered a pitcher I had seen, made from broken chards of china. I decided I could make one of those from the broken pieces of my mother's china.

The process was long and arduous as I tried to fit and glue little pieces of cream and turquoise chards together into a mosaic around a glass pitcher frame. I went to the Thrift Shop and found a couple of flowered china cups that, broken, I could use to make into a heart design in the middle of the bowl. I made something beautiful, lasting and fit to remember my mother. My china fragments had become a pitcher that represented not only her love but God's gift of healing all our brokenness.

Brokenness happens to all of us, and we are as fragile as china plates. I bring my pitcher to retreats to help remind others of their fragility, and how Spirit can put us back together more beautiful than we ever were.

The Energetic System and Prayer

Ancient Eastern understandings of the energetic body system have been very helpful in treating sources of illness and brokenness. In the last century, Westerners have discovered that working with the energetic system provides an added dimension to modern medicine. Its function is both preventive and curative. Mostly, it is holistic, meaning that it works with each of the levels of the body's energy. I was trained as a Healing Therapist through Catholic Health Initiatives at our local hospital as a way to expand my work as a spiritual director.

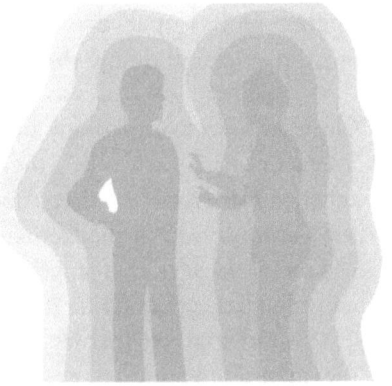

Layers of the human energy field extend beyond the physical body.

The complete body has an interconnected system of energy vortexes which work at various levels: i.e., etheric (physical), mental, emotional, and spiritual. In it there are seven major vortexes, called chakras.[12] These vortexes extend beyond the physical body through each layer and can be "massaged" by a trained therapist. When the therapist opens a vortex closed by negative energy, the healthy flow of the energy resumes within the related organs, flooding them with renewed energy to heal. Our bodies can heal themselves when the energy systems are open. Recognize that our body is a complex system that encompasses much more than we can see. Spirit's energy is a part of our body in a way that can deeply influence our healing. Trained energy practitioners in Healing Touch, Reiki, and Healing Therapy are well-adept at feeling and differentiating each layer.

When we grieve, we shut down some of those vortexes at the emotional level, and we place ourselves in danger of imbalance. Unacknowledged and unaddressed grief doesn't just evaporate, however. It often turns into real anxiety, depression, even illness. Feelings of sadness, which are often overwhelming, must be consciously addressed, using energy therapy, counseling, journaling, and other ways of becoming self-aware.

Perhaps unbeknownst to him, preacher and a physicist John Polkinghorrne has opened a window on prayer with his explanation of quantum particles and how they interact.

> Once two electrons (or any other pair of quantum particles) have interacted with each other, they possess a power to influence each other, however widely they subsequently separate. If one electron stays around here in the laboratory and the other goes 'beyond the Moon' (as we say), then anything I do to the electron here will have an immediate effect on its distant brother. In other words, there's a very surprising 'togetherness in separation' built in to the fabric of the quantum world.[13]

Our prayers are energy directed at God. We are part of a creation where each of our energies are actually connected through God. Our prayers can have immediate effect on the person or situation we are praying for. This is made quite visible in Healing Therapy practice, when we engage in "long distance healing," as though the person we were working on, even thousands of miles away, were lying on the massage table in our room. When we center and focus on that person, our movements (either in our minds or physically) open that person for healing. If I live in New York and I am working on a person in California, the transfer of energy will not be delayed by the speed of light or sound, because life energy is immediate. Practitioners have found that long distance treatment is as effective as treatment in person.

One of the miraculous ways our body functions is through our autonomic nervous system. We have no conscious control over it, but day in and day out it keeps us breathing, keeps our heart pumping and makes our organs function regularly. Our breath is the only of those autonomic functions that we can take control over for moments. With the Psalmist, I am constantly amazed at what the body can do, especially after I experienced open heart surgery not long ago.

> For you created my inmost being;
> you knit me together in my mother's womb.
> I praise you because I am fearfully and wonderfully made;
> your works are wonderful,
> I know that full well.
> My frame was not hidden from you
> when I was made in the secret place.
> When I was woven together in the depths of the earth,
> your eyes saw my unformed body.[14]

Wholeness vs. Wellness

Good health can be thought of as the process of harmony and right relationship in a person. We are all responsible for and capable of positively influencing our community, our environment or our own situation. Changing ourselves or our environment begins within, with our healthy thinking and lifestyles.

Although it is true that our choices in life influence our health, other influences play a major role that we may have very little control over. Genetic inheritance leads the way in determining our weak spots, whether it be heart, bones, digestion, or any disease that is hereditary. I used to tease my parents that *all because of them*, I had to have sinus and stomach troubles. Little did I know at that time that I had also inherited their heart problems. Back then I didn't even realize that their heart histories would have a great influence on my own heart history. The sad thing is that my children have received those same genes, which will continue to be passed on to generations to come without some amazing intervention that science or lifestyle changes can provide. Growing older is never without complications, and our only recourse is to respect ourselves and treat our bodies, minds and spirits the best we can before they have a chance to become sick.

What are we asking when we ask to be healed? Our English word, *heal* is derived from the old English *Haelen*, the Germanic *Herlein* and the Greek *Holos*, which mean, "To make sound or whole." Holistic healing implies more than bodily restoration, as its meaning expands to become a transformational process encompassing body, mind and spirit. It actually signifies a restoration to wholeness. As a movement toward health, harmony and wholeness, healing implies a change of spiritual outlook. We must learn to re-pattern and align ourselves to higher levels of functioning in our choices and relationships. Holistically, we learn to take responsibility for our health and wellness, so that we can experience wholeness in health or *even* in illness.

Our word *cure* is derived from the Latin, *cura*, which means care of souls. Cure is an action which corrects, heals or alleviates a harmful or troublesome situation. Wholeness encompasses more than cure and is the true goal of healing.[15]

Therapy is not the same as healing. "At its root, *therapy* derives from a word meaning 'to hold up and support.'[16] Although therapy is useful, therapeutic, and rational thinking may not touch the secret place inside us where we harbor the ability to change our lives. Ultimately, our healing will come from within.

Harmony and balance are signs of healing. Energy therapists practicing Healing Touch or Healing Therapy work with body energy to restore harmony and balance. The work is a spiritual process, because it is done through the centered heart, based on unconditional love. In the stance of unconditional love, the therapist is open to the other without expectation, with the intention for their highest good. Jesus performed his miracles of healing with this unconditional love, expressing his union with God. When he forgave their sins, it was a sign of unconditional love. Love heals. This is a mystical thought, and when a "healer" experiences the deep energy connections she has made, it can only be explained as a mystical action that is made possible by the grace of God.

Disease, on the other hand, is described by two Chinese characters, literally meaning sickness and soul, which implies that *disease is a sickness of the soul.* Dis-ease implies an imbalance or disruption within. The traditional western medical approach is symptom removal, which does not always provide healing in the broader, holistic sense. Often, surgeries simply require deeper healing.

We can be born or later afflicted with certain conditions that preclude a "normal life," and we must choose how we will live the life we have been given – whether we see it as disabled or as differently-abled. Each of us must live with who we are – our spiritual as well as physical essence. Our ability to love and respect ourselves just as we are will bring us miles closer to being whole than if we can't accept a condition that cannot be changed. Wholeness is not wellness. Wellness is the absence of disease. Wholeness is the presence of the Spirit with love and respect for ourself and others.

Breath

I stated earlier that the breath we take is Spirit entering us and assuring life. It is involuntary, like a flood of water pushing through a dam under the pressure of a flood. We don't ask for it; we simply receive it. Our response is to let that air flow through us and then breathe it out. Breath controls our life and even health, and it is the source of our energy.

Have you noticed that, when you are under stress, your breathing changes? Some of us (like me) unconsciously hold our breath when we feel stressed. Holding the breath stops the flow of that energy through our bodies. We don't notice what we're doing, but our body does. "Hey, where's the air? I need it!" the body tries to say. Our organs do a little dance of "Feed me, feed me," and the whole system gets out of rhythm. We have less energy, we are less alert, we slow down to a kind of not feeling well but not sick. Sound familiar?

I once went to a biofeedback doctor to see what he could do to help my blood pressure go down. He figured out very quickly that I had been holding my breath when I was under stress, and that I needed to learn how to consciously breathe more deeply and more regularly. This in turn would affect my blood pressure. I stuck a little red dot on my computer to remind me to breathe deeply every hour. I even set a wristwatch alarm to remind me to breathe deeply. It helped.

Andrew Weil, M.D., has offered breathing lessons to people who are suffering from circulation problems or many other ailments. I will share one of his techniques here, because it has been helpful to me and so many others. The two exercises start with a short breath huffing and puffing from the chest through the nose with your mouth closed, as fast as you can, for a count up to 15. Keep your tongue at the top of your mouth behind your front teeth during these exercises. The next exercise involves holding the breath and then letting it out slowly. Take a slow deep breath for four counts. Hold that breath for seven counts, and then open your lips and exhale slowly for eight counts. Do four repetitions of this exercise.

These techniques are good when you under a lot of stress – late for an appointment, angry that something hasn't gone the way you wanted—common stresses. The short period of concentrated breathing break will help open the heart chakra again, so that it can beat regularly and fully, so that the blood can flow freely through the body.

We all have unconscious habits that can contribute to making us sick. Without awareness of these habits, we can never change them. Become aware of what your body is saying to you! Be aware of your breath!

Stress

Stress can be good or bad, but either way, it will affect our health if we're in it for prolonged periods. When it's good, we don't mind being stressed out because we're getting married, or we're in love, or we got a promotion. Those aren't bad things, but they can interrupt our breathing and tense the body. "Bad" stress can come from our grief, anger or hatred, or even busy-ness that keeps us from paying attention to what our body needs. Any kind of stress can use some intervention of relaxation and compassion.

The stress response is automatically connected with the fight or flight response that our Creator built into our survival instincts. Sometimes we need the extra push to get away from a threat, or to do whatever it takes to stay safe. When the stress response occurs, adrenaline flows will throw us off-balance and may stretch long beyond the threat before the body's reactions can return to normal. In that time, the entire physical system begins to break down, and our immune systems are disrupted. Symptoms can include headache, muscle tightness, faster breathing, higher heart rate, increased blood pressure, indigestion, stomachache, dilated pupils, sweaty hands, fatigue, trouble sleeping, negative thoughts, decreased concentration.

Have you ever wondered why you got a bad viral infection, when your spouse or your friend who has been exposed to the same virus is perfectly fine? You don't have to feel guilty about your body's allowing the virus to activate sickness in you, but you do need to be aware that something within you was weakening your immune system so that your body could not fight the threat of illness. Was it stress? What can you do about that? Self-awareness can be used to prevent many illnesses.

Your body is an enormous healing machine. Every day it fights off a multitude of threats to your health, and you have no idea how efficient it is. It is only when you succumb to illness that you take the time to consider what is weakening your body. Attitude and emotion are important aspects of the effectiveness of your healing machine. Disappointment, depression, and discouragement work their way through your body to weaken your system. To combat these attacks, Spirit is working in you to give you hope and courage to change parts of your life that are making you sick.

It is important to know how to respond to stress by relaxing and releasing your muscle tension. Slow down your breathing and let go of worries and negative thoughts. These four steps will help: *Stop. Breathe. Reflect/Pray, Choose.* Spirit would say, "Choose to love." When you let Spirit in to help you deal with your stress, it will make all the difference.

Letting Go, Forgiveness

The rational techniques that we use to relieve stress cannot help if we tenaciously hold on to anger or hatred or resentment or hurt. When we have been hurt deeply, it's easy to carry it on our shoulders like heavy armor. That feeling also adds to our shell and closes our heart to the love of Spirit – not just for the other person, but for ourselves. Think about how good it would feel to your body not to have to carry that weight around all the time.

"But I feel justified in my anger. He was a horrible person. He hurt me!"

Sorry, but your anger is hurting you more than it is hurting him. Even righteous anger poisons our systems. Letting go of it by forgiving is what starts the emotional as well as physical healing process. Fifty years ago, Agnes Sanford, the healer, said that when we give way to anger, the "protective and life-giving forces of the body are weakened so that one falls prey to germs and infections, to pain and weakness, to nervousness and ill temper, and to the spiritual dullness that results from the dimming of the life force." [17]

Forgiveness is not new. Jesus told us we were to forgive seven times seventy times. The only thing that is stronger than forgiveness is love. Mrs. Sanford recommends when confronted with someone who makes you angry, simply send them love. Love never fails. But that's easier said than done.

It helps to look at the anger rationally. Make a list of what is keeping you from forgiving: wanting revenge, wanting to punish, wanting justice, wanting to look superior, wanting …. It's your list.

The anger originates in our shell, our outward life, not in our inward life. In the inward life, we hear Spirit saying, "I love you so very much. I am so sorry you were hurt. But I love him, too. I want him to learn to love. I'm working in you to help you learn to love each other."

If you really heard that in your heart, would you respond from your heart and let the shell go? That is what Spirit is asking and helping you to do. Forgiveness is something you may never be able to do on your own, but Spirit can make it possible.

Sometimes the person who is hardest to forgive is yourself. That anger comes from the shell as well. "I'm not good enough, I always make mistakes, I always say the wrong thing, I'm such an idiot." We are so hard on ourselves, especially when our perfectionist archetype rears its nagging head. I wrote about kicking myself early in my life, since evidently, I needed it.

Kicking Myself

Never forget the mistake – never let it pass.
Live it on and over until it's grey and tattered,
Sicker, uglier, more despicable.
Torture is no sweet recompense for a sickened soul.
If God forgives, why can't I?
God, help me to love myself!

Love is the answer. It always is. *God is love, and anyone who is living in love is living in God, and God is living in him.* (1 John 4:16b) Accessing this love is a process of opening to Spirit, letting down our defensive shell, and letting go. Here are some steps you can take to practice forgiveness.

1. Pray for the grace to forgive.
2. See the person as a child of God who is loved and forgiven.
3. Try to understand what made them the way they are.
4. Ask what their presence in your life has taught you. (Are you stronger, wiser, more or less courageous?)
5. In a spirit of compassion, ask God to heal them of their twisted lives.
6. Send them love from God and from your heart, even if you don't feel it.

Practice and Ideas to Ponder

1. Do this activity to experience the invisible layers of energy that surround your body.

    a. First, rub your hands together vigorously. Now hold them a few inches apart, palms facing each other, and bounce them in and out. When you feel energy between your palms, move your hands further out and pretend that there is a ball between them. Let the ball grow larger as you feel the pull of the energy when you enlarge the distance between your hands and widen your fingers. Where do you think this energy ball came from?

    b. Now, with a friend, do the same by resting your hand on their shoulder and then backing your hand off the shoulder a few inches. What do you feel? Can you feel the same thing as you move your hand down their arm?

2. Write a prayer to ask for help in accepting yourself as you are. Ask God for the wisdom and ability to love yourself in concrete ways of care, attention, and awareness.

3. Exercise to center on your breath and relax.

   a. Sit comfortably with good posture, spine straight, shoulders relaxed.
   b. Place a hand on your chest to feel for movement of the rib cage muscles. There should be little or no movement of the upper chest when you breathe.
   c. Place the other hand in the middle of your abdomen to feel for movement. Your hand should rise with the inhalation and lower with exhalation.
   d. Pull your abdominal muscles in as you exhale slowly through your nose or mouth.
   e. Inhale through your nose, feeling your abdomen rise and move out to the front.
   f. As you breathe deeply, let your breath in symbolize the presence of God coming into your heart, saying, "I love you, ____." As you breathe out, let your breath symbolize, "I love you, God."

4. When have you had trouble forgiving someone? What was your *physical* experience? What if the person hurt you so deeply that you don't think you can possibly forgive? How have you tried? Will you try again?

5. Practice the six steps in forgiving on a person you find difficult to forgive. Go over this several days in a row. Record what you have experienced.

6. How do you punish yourself? What do you think Spirit is saying to you?

CHAPTER 5

Growing Your Spirit

It is he whom we proclaim, warning everyone and teaching everyone in all wisdom, so that we may present everyone mature in Christ.

Colossians 1:28 NRSV

When you were born, you were as close to being a whole person as you will ever be. The essence of who you are is in your soul, your unique identity that God created in you. It is connected intimately with and knows God. This is where God lives with you, where you are totally free of the shell that has distorted who you are. Your wholeness as a baby does not mean that you knew everything and understood everything at that stage of life. Wholeness not about intelligence nor even about perfection, especially when perfection seems unattainable.

Wholeness is a life-long journey because the short period of innocence of the baby is soon over, and life interferes with our trust and even our awareness. Just when we think we've got it together, we fall apart. We grow up, and we lose our connection to God. Acting from our shell, we say and do things that aren't loving or respectful. We don't recognize souls in the people we don't get along with. We wage war with friends as well as enemies, all for the sake of self-interest, getting our piece of the pie. We especially disdain people who don't think or believe like we do. We judge them from our own position: They're different. They think differently—they don't even have a soul!

The problem is that's not how God made us. God made us out of love so that we could love one another. Only in connection with our Creator can we find our way to become the loving, balanced and harmonious person we were meant to be. Only in connection with Spirit can we learn how to help others be the persons they were meant to be. Breaking out of the Divided Life is a life-long process of adulthood. So, the stages of life are not just *innocence* and then *adulthood*. They are multi-faceted shaded stages of maturity that shine from our Spirit and are reflected in all we say and do.

Mature in Christ

It is he whom we proclaim, warning everyone and teaching everyone in all wisdom, so that we may present everyone mature in Christ.

Colossians 1:28

Every Man — Every Woman
We have to grow up
open up, give up
our old natures
those wretched, tangled knots
of self-protection
mixed with self-rejection...
Who wants them, anyway?
Jesus, you can have mine.
My knots are so cumbersome, so heavy

I hate them more and more as I become aware of them!
And you can resurrect them
into the new ME
that only I can be
through you
through God's love in you.

In Christ let me mature,
Growing up all at once,
Yet a little more each day...
Learning his way, hearing his word
feeling his prodding
Responding to his voice, thanking him endlessly
in snuffled undertones
brilliant overtones
of *Joy, Love, Peace, Patience, Faithfulness, Hope,
Kindness, Self-Control*

For his *Gift*
For my *Map* to maturity.
O Lord, thank you!

Jesus became impatient with the Pharisees of his time and quoted the Old Testament in his frustrations with them:

> You will be indeed listening, but never understand.
> You will indeed look, but never perceive.
> For this people's heart has grown dull.
> and their ears are hard of hearing,
> and they have shut their eyes
> so that they might not look with their eyes
> and listen with their ears,
> and understand with their heart and turn--
> and I would heal them.
>   [Matthew 13:13-16, NRSV]

In this scripture, we are to think of the word "heal" in the context of turning back to God. Turn away from what is making us "sick." In this sense this is just like the concept of sin and repentance. Normally, we think of healing as physical, but whole healing reflects who we are in mind, body and Spirit. Our inner journey will make possible our outward journey. If we live only outside the shell, we have no resources to live into the questions and make sense of the paradoxes that make doing God's will so fruitful to our souls.

Healing means we learn to live *through* the paradoxes of life with renewed attitudes:

- Learn Humility. Jesus told us that to be strong we must be weak. Bullies don't have the edge in Spirit's realm.
- Trust. Pain can be a pathway to joy—look at Jesus' death and resurrection.
- Be Open. To be great we must become like little children.
- Be Creative & Flexible. Move through the chaos and confusion of life and emerge in clarity, newness, and even beauty.

To work through those paradoxes, our life journey needs to be made in the company of Spirit and people who are on the same quest as we are – to know God and live the authentic life. That is why we gather in communities of faith and find spiritual companions—persons who can share our journey. Our spiritual companions help us soften our shells, as we help them soften theirs. When we don't have those companions, we seek out a spiritual director who will listen to our heart and point us toward the heart of God.

Jesus was a spiritual director to the rich man who came to him asking, "Teacher, what must I do to receive eternal life?" Please note that Jesus didn't tell him what to do right away. Jesus reminded him of the law of Moses, which the rich man recognized and recited by rote: "You must love the Lord your God with all your heart, all your soul, all your strength, and all your mind, and love your neighbor as yourself." And Jesus replied, "You have answered correctly." Do this and you will live."[18] Jesus knew that the man had the answer to his question inside him and only sought to draw it out. The companioning process, working with a spiritual guide, always opens the pathway to discovering the answers inside yourself.

When we love God with all our soul, Spirit is free to direct our strength and our mind. Only then can we see the soul in the other and learn to love it and honor it as well. Our spirituality, based on our relationship to God, will include prayer as well as love in action, as we respond to the Spirit moving in us.

Most people think of spirituality as being entirely feeling-based, but we know that there are as many types of spirituality as there are personality types, as evidenced in Enneagram studies. One theoretician has approached spirituality and religion from an entirely integrated stance, examining psychological, scientific, philosophical and spiritual traditions. Ken Wilbur's **Integral Spirituality** unites all the major spiritual traditions to understand the progressive journey of the human spirit toward wholeness, or unity with God.

Using four quadrants of human consciousness, Wilbur demonstrates how we are more than the sum of our parts: body, mind and spirit. What we are and do all together make up our integral spirituality. In his analysis, we operate in four modes of understanding:

- The Subjective/Internal
- Objective /Physical
- Cultural/Inter-Subjective
- The Social (or Inter-Objective)

When these modes are in balance, we are more whole or more integrated in our thoughts and actions and can progress in our spiritual understandings. Wholeness is actually integrating all our lives in order to be the person we were created to be. Spirit encompasses all of who we are. I have simplified his deep and detailed scientific study to this barebones approach.

Wilbur's Four Quadrants[19]

Subjective/Internal Meditation, Prayer, Breath Work/Singing, Study, Writing, Journaling	**Objective/Physical** Medications, Diet, Walking, Weight Training, Aerobics, Yoga, Dance, Sleep, Diet
Subjective/External Family, Small Groups, Church Worship, Community Service, Volunteer Work	**Inter-Objective** Recycling, Teaching, Gardening, Political Support, Memberships

[19:] © Wilbur, K. (2006). *Integral Spirituality, A Startling New Role for Religion in the Modern and Postmodern World.* Boston and London: Integral Books.

The Subjective/Internal Quadrant

When we are in the upper left quadrant, the Subjective/Internal mode, we focus on ourselves in an interior process of observation and self-awareness. This quadrant represents your awareness, both internal and external, of your stages and states of consciousness—your inner realizations and spiritual experiences. This is your emotional, spiritual, visionary life. We do certain things in this mode, such as meditate, pray, sing, study, write, or journal.

Singing or even listening to music can help tune us to Spirit without much effort. Scientists have discovered that certain tones resonate in our bodies with a fullness that can help us relax, open our minds and even heal. Meditation accompanied with a background of music composed for these tones to sink deep within can be highly effective, especially if you have a hard time focusing.[19]

Journaling is a way to record your spiritual needs and attitudes so that you can learn from insights you may have. I have often thought of my journaling as more revealing than periods of meditation because there is something concrete that comes of it. The words stay with me. Sometimes I write poems which always astonish me with their insights. I know that this is a deep communication in Spirit with the Divine, and I treasure those gifts that have come my way. But first, I must be quiet, go within, and listen.

For many people, the internal quadrant is neglected for more external activities. Our busy schedules and sociability keep us from taking time to center into our core, even as we know that not going within could result in living the Divided Life, disconnected from our God-created essence.

Rarely, some are so interiorly oriented that they disconnect with the externals. It is easier for an introverted person to work in this Subjective/Internal area, but we extroverts can learn. Trying to center my Enneagram Type 7 personality into such a quiet time can be a major effort! Journaling finally focused me and kept me from all my distractions. Wholeness requires this focus, and we can all find ways to make inner spiritual consciousness a solid part of living.

The Subjective External Quadrant

In the lower left quadrant lies the Subjective/External mode of our lives, where we approach who we are on the inside as an objective or scientific observer, with the help of others. When you make an effort to see yourself as others see you, or even to understand others from your perspective, you are interpreting how you come together with other "I"s to make a "We". Perspective is completely personal, because no one else has your perspective – not even your twin sister! What we see and think about things depends entirely on who we are, whom we have known and what has happened to us. "We" is sometimes an enormous challenge because of the chasm of perspective that truly exists between ourselves and others.

Where do you come together with another person to become "we" – sharing Spirit and learning from each other? This is a place where religious groups can be so helpful, as they offer activities of worship, small group work, community service and volunteer work. If your religious community is already divided by quarrels or factions, it can't serve this role efficiently. The group you share Spirit with must be worthy of your trust.

This quadrant requires a listening, compassionate ear, and the willingness to be yourself and share your questions and insights. This quadrant could include therapy and counseling, even family interactions – any group that is serious about understanding their relationship through the Spirit. If you live in a family, each member must work in this quadrant for the health of the family so that together you can grow in your spiritual understandings. Children need this outlet for their wisely innocent spiritual observations, and your receptive spirit will help keep them open to it.

The Objective/Physical Quadrant

On the right side of the diagram is your external activity and work. The upper right quadrant is the Objective/Physical mode, which includes the activities you do to take care of yourself, such as conventional or alternative medicine, diet, walking, aerobics, sleep, etc. Yes, this is a part of your spiritual self which will contribute to your understanding of your life in the world. When we are "stuck" in this quadrant, we allow others to determine how we should care for our mental and physical health and do not take personal responsibility. The balanced understanding of this quadrant must relate to our internal spiritual consciousness (of the left quadrants) as we interact with physical caring and concerns. When we allow self-awareness through spiritual centering of the left quadrants, we add in the elements of internal healing powers that will help us experience peace and let go.

An individual's energy healing would not fall in this Objective/Physical quadrant, because it is an internal/external subjective work with the Spirit. However, the energy practitioner's work on another is a part of their own objective/physical spirituality, in the upper right quadrant. Also, when you are doing energy healing on yourself, it is in the upper left quadrant, and when someone does it on you, it is in the lower left quadrant.

How we care for our bodies is fundamental to a spiritually full life. Sickness and pain drain our spirits, deplete our energy, and depress our perspective. Allopathic (conventional) Western medical traditions use drugs to relieve symptoms. The medications do not really work to heal what is causing the pain, but they allow more normal activity than when we are beset with pain. Sometimes we do need to ease the pain before we can work at its root.

For instance, people with back pain want to find relief, and so they take pain pills. Medical choices are complicated because some drugs are harmful to other parts of the body. Some pain pills have been found to be destructive to the kidneys. Others, taken in too large doses, can destroy the liver! The intelligent patient must understand what he is doing to his body when he eats certain foods or takes certain medications. This quadrant requires vigilance and self-discipline if the body is to be cared for holistically.

A spiritual understanding of the physical body is why alternative medical treatments have been passed down through the centuries and can serve as complementary and integrative therapies to western medicine. There is much wisdom in yoga practices, Tai Chi, homeopathy, chiropractic, osteopathy, acupuncture and other complementary treatments. The wisdom of what to use and when becomes your decision, as you listen to and love your body into wellness, and ultimately wholeness.

Most important, you must love your body, and not look at yourself as too fat, too thin, ugly, or unattractive. Women particularly obsess over imperfections, especially growing old. How many new wrinkle creams come out every year? But we are who God made us to be, and wholeness comes as we learn to accept who we are. Our habits of putting ourselves down are not habits of humility. They come from self-hate, not from self-love. Replace those habits with positive thoughts of what you know needs to change for better health. You can make the most of what you have and not be pulled down into the rabbit hole of self-rejection. If you were born with one arm, you still have the other, and you are a whole person by your acceptance of being a person with one arm and doing your best to live successfully with what you have.

The Social (or Inter-Objective)

In the lower right quadrant is your Social and Inter-Objective mode, which includes the cultural, social and economic systems that make it possible for you to function as a person in society. How you interact spiritually within that system forms a congruent life with yourself and others. You may choose to recycle to conserve resources.

Now

Not past
Not yet
Now
A time to be
A time to listen
A time to watch

Doing will be done
Didn't doesn't count
Not today.

Today brings silence
Waiting
Sensing
Soaking in the sounds of creation

God's activity
Clothes my mind
In reflection
NOW

Turtle Rock Farm: A Center for Sustainability, Spirituality and Healing, is a retreat center in Oklahoma, led by spiritual directors who know the importance of connecting your spirit with creation. When groups or individuals of any age come to spend time there, they experience the rising and the setting of the sun, learn how to work with the soil, plant their own vegetables, and spend the day soaking in the gifts of creation. Their motto is, "It is God (Creator) who is the spiritual director."[20] In this place, participants experience God all around them and within them. They receive revelation in very deep ways. Their eyes are opened to their connection with all of creation. This is a picture of spirituality in the external fourth quadrant.

Other fourth quadrant activities may include teaching, so that others may learn important values in society, but also that you can learn more about the people you teach. You may form political or social alliances that conform to your basic values in life. These alliances will set you on a journey of understanding what is basic to social relationships you value. Your choices reflect who you are as a child of God. These activities are aways spiritual exercises when the activity points your spirit in directions of growth and expansion.

When your choices are disconnected with who you are, however, you deplete your spirit and disintegrate your life, creating the Divided Life. Choices of how you spend your time should reflect your values and your perspectives. As we mature, we hope that our choices improve, because we are all growing toward integration of our spirit and our outward life. Life lived earnestly in this area will help you grow to understand others and yourself.

Maturing in Spirit requires a quieted mind and focused activity. That seems to be an oxymoron, but it is the art of living/dancing in the presence of the Spirit. First, find your quiet place or time, even schedule it, then find people you want to share your journey. Choose healthy practices for your body, and then find the passion of your soul – activities that will express who you are. Your life can be a gift to all creation.

Practice and Ideas to Ponder

1. Describe yourself as a 10-year-old.

   What was your passion?
   What did you think of yourself?
   What did you hope to become?

2. Describe a relationship with someone who is a spiritual partner with you. Why is this person a good fit with you? If you don't have one, describe a relationship that you would like to help you grow in your spiritual understandings.

3. Fill in the chart below, developed by Ken Wilbur, with the activities you engage in for each quadrant (see examples on page 59).

My Wholeness Chart

Subjective/Internal	Objective/Physical
Subjective/External	Inter-Objective

4. Which quadrant needs more attention in contributing to your wholeness? Why?

5. How do you see yourself maturing in your spirituality today?

CHAPTER 6

Stages of Spiritual Consciousness

For you were once darkness, but now you are light in the Lord.
Live as children of light (for the fruit of the light consists in all goodness,
righteousness and truth) and find out what pleases the Lord.

Ephesians 5:8-9 *NIV*

Spiritual growth is the path to wholeness. Spirituality is a part of who we are, not dependent on what religion we follow. It is true, Christian spirituality uniquely includes the presence and leadership of Jesus Christ in our lives, but people of all the major religions worship, pray or meditate, and act in congruence with their spiritual values. Ken Wilbur has created a developmental line to identify stages of human spiritual consciousness. It starts at the most primal level (tribal) and ascends through the process of personal growth and maturity through seven stages to transcendency. He has assigned symbolic colors to each of these stages—colors which also correspond to energy centers in the body. Here we have a scientific study that connects us with centuries-old understandings of the body. Combining these two approaches in a holistic view of our health makes possible new insights into what wholeness really is.

The Chakra System

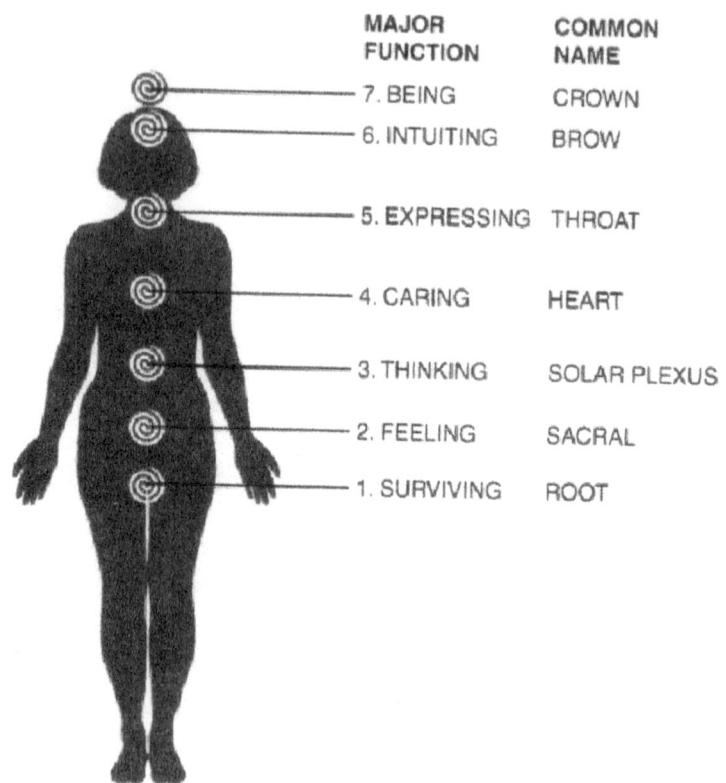

In several of her books, most notably **Anatomy of the Spirit**, medical intuitive Caroline Myss has done extensive work to understand and clarify our body's energy system for healing. This energy system is ancient and has been recognized in almost every culture of our world, although with different names. Myss identifies seven points of the chakra (energy) system of the body, and Ken Wilbur's spiritual stages studies coincide with the path of seven chakras of the body.[21] My synthesis, or interpretation, creates an opportunity for deeper understanding, I believe, of a person's growth and evolution in spiritual consciousness, wholeness, and health. I encourage you to read more about these centers of energy in detail from both Wilbur and Myss.

The Chakra System[22]

A person's spiritual stage necessarily limits his spiritual consciousness to that level or below. You cannot function from a level to which you have not matured, and so you must mature through each one to get to the next stage. The Wilbur-Combs Lattice pictures a matrix that compares *stages*/levels of spirituality with the spiritual *states* experienced. He notes that a person can have a peak spiritual experience, but her interpretation of it will depend on what stage she is in (her understanding of who she is in relationship with the world).[23]

I have combined the Wilbur-Combs Lattice with Caroline Myss' description of each of the energy centers (chakras) of the body to give us a whole picture of how our spirituality is formed.

Synthesis of Ken Wilbur's *Stages of Spiritual Consciousness* and Carolyn Myss' *Anatomy of the Spirit*

Chakra Title	Color	Self Identity	Primary Spiritual Task	Stage of Faith	Worldview
7 Crown	Clear light/ Ultra Violet/ Violet	Transpersonal/ Transcendent	Union with God	Openness	Universal
6 Mind	Indigo	High Vision-Logic/ Ego-Aware	Detachment	Universalizing	Integral
5 Throat	Turquoise/ Sky Blue	Integrated/ Autonomous	Align with the Will of God	Commonwealth	Pluralistic
4 Heart	Green	Individualistic/ Conscientious	Love Unconditionally	Conjunctive	Rational
3 Solar Plexus	Yellow/ Light Orange	Conformist	Develop Self-Esteem	Individual-Reflexive	Mythic
2 Sacrum	Orange/ Amber	Impulsive	Live in Relation-ships	Conventional	Magic
1 Root	Red/ Magenta	Symbiotic/ Survival	Protect the Tribe	Mythic-Literal/ Undifferentiated/ Magical	Magic/ Archaic

First Chakra – The Root

The first energy center in our body represents our human beginnings. The Spirit in this chakra is concerned with group loyalty for the survival of the "tribe." This area, located at the base, of the spine, the coccyx, is called the Root Chakra. Each chakra has a symbolic color which can be seen in energy scans such as the CT scan, but it can also be seen in the meditative imagination/vision. The color of this chakra is shades of red – symbolizing blood lines, war and power. We start our lives with the blood lines of our ancestry and the culture we grow up in. The spiritual stage of the first chakra is life in a world that uses magic to interpret things we don't understand. Our trust is in our ancient tribal wisdom."[24] Our entire identity is in our tribe, and our worldview does not go beyond it.

In our body, the root chakra affects our spinal column, rectum, legs, bones, feet and immune system. The emotional and psychological issues that find their home here are basic to our mental health, because the family unit and the early social environment are our anchor in life.[25] Just like a tree or a plant, we bloom when we are planted in good soil and grow strong from it. If the soil has been lacking, we need extra care and nurture to make up for it. Our roots determine how hard or easy life will be in most circumstances.

First chakra thinking is very literal, with little or no symbolism. It relies on structure and logic to keep the world in order. When we are in the first chakra, we take events and relationships at face value, with little nuance. Things are black and white, good or bad. The tribe (family) is the anchor; outsiders are threats.

The tribal culture shares a connection with all of human life, and each member is a part of the whole. *All is One* is the conscious mentality, rather than the *Individual*. Shared belief and moral and ethical codes include both wisdom and superstition handed down from generations. Children start at this place in their development, and many, many people remain here in their spiritual consciousness. The primary spiritual task of this stage is to protect the tribe. It demands uniformity to the code at all cost.

This chakra is where war originates—in the body and in the world around us. Loyalty, membership, defense and honor form the basic values, while anger, revenge, hatred, bigotry thrive. Only when crisis comes can the tribal attitudes recognize that something needs to be changed.

In our personal spiritual development, crisis will also make us examine what needs to change in our lives and make it possible to progress in our spiritual consciousness.

Physically, the immune system does for the body what the survival code of the tribe does to fend off invasion. When outside threats appear, and the "war" is being lost, a victim consciousness can develop, and the body will succumb to powerlessness. In our own bodies, the knees give out, the immune system breaks down, and we become sick. In the same way, our spirit can become sick unless we can grow to see beyond inherent tribal teachings to a deeper level of truth.

> Carl Jung once remarked that the group mind is the "lowest" form of consciousness because individuals involved in a negative group action rarely, if ever, accept responsibility for their personal role and action. This reality is the shadow side of the truth *All Is One*.[26]

When we consider the behavior of the Nazis accused of genocide against the Jews after World War II, we see this clearly. Their defense was, "We were only following orders." This is typical of the first chakra and the first spiritual stage of consciousness. A person in a lower stage cannot see beyond it. He will use his tradition alone in his reasoning process. Only by spiritual enlightenment can he move out of this stage and into the next.

Second Chakra – The Sacrum

Wilbur's research reveals the next stage of consciousness, still in the first tier, as "Ego-centric and Self-Protecting."[27] This stage corresponds to Myss' understanding of the Second Chakra, located just above the Root Chakra in the Sacrum.

The sacrum includes all the organs located between the lower abdomen and the navel area and is the center of power in our relationships. Since our reproductive organs are in this area, the ultimate ability to create a new life becomes an option to us as we stand at the door of creative energy. The color of this center is orange, which symbolizes our creative powers represented by choice, "the process of creation itself."[28] We begin to individualize and create, and our primary task is to live in relationship with others.

About the time we reach the age of seven, we become more aware of how we relate to others and the world and explore our power of choice and creativity. The need to control the dynamics of our physical environment originates in this area of the body. Disorders of the reproductive system and lower spine often reflect distress and fear for creative ambition in the business world and at home. Here is where our fight or flight reflex and our ability to take risks for survival are felt. As Caroline Myss teaches.

> The challenge of the second chakra is to learn what motivates us to make the choices we do. In learning about our motivations, we learn about the content of our spirits. Are you filled with fear, or are you filled with faith? Every choice we make contains the energy of either faith or fear, and the outcome of every decision reflects to some extent that faith or fear. This dynamic of choice guarantees that we cannot run away from ourselves or our decisions.[29]

The sacred truth of the Second Chakra is *Honor One Another*.[30] As we ourselves differentiate from the tribe to live as individuals, we struggle to learn to live in relationship with others. Life gets more complicated. As we learn to live in relationship, we learn to respect the other. Our interactions must be considered in the light of what control we are willing to give up. We grow in spiritual wisdom as we value relationships with others.

Whereas in the first stage of spiritual consciousness the only choice was the tribe, living from the second chakra means a duality involving relationships, especially trying to get along with them and deal with feelings of rejection and acceptance. We spend most of our early development in this second stage. You will recognize the feelings of the adolescent trying to live creatively and assert his independence. In this second stage, he begins to enlarge his boundaries beyond family.

My friend, Susie, had two bad marriages. Her first husband abused her physically, but her second husband abused her mentally. He told her she was not worth anything because she hadn't been able to get pregnant. Getting out of those relationships was essential to her health, but years later she still carried around her hurt for not having children and her anger at the men who had not stood by her when she needed their support. Finally, at age 55, she found out she had ovarian cancer. The tumor was as big as a cantaloupe. She was scared.

Susie came to me willing to try anything to get rid of that "alien baby" inside her, and she sought out energy therapists she knew. I gave her a session of Healing Therapy, and I organized a healing prayer service for her. During one treatment, we talked about why she called the tumor an "alien baby." She admitted her disappointment over never having a baby and how she resented the men in her life. I told her that the location of the tumor did reflect her feelings, for it is in the sacrum area of her body that reproduction takes place. I asked her to pray and think about what connection this had to her life experiences.

The great thing about Susie was that she was willing to examine her feelings and pray and journal about them, so that she came to understand the physical affect that her anger was producing in her body. By the time we had the prayer service, as each of her friends told her how much she meant to them, and as we prayed for healing, she had a spiritual awakening. Susie said she left that service feeling wrapped in a golden cocoon, quieting her spirit and assuring her of how loved she was. It was this cocoon that kept her grounded in God's love as she went into the surgery.

After the surgery, the doctor was amazed, because the tumor had broken free of her ovary and fallen down into the pelvic wall. It had collapsed upon itself. The biopsy showed that the cells were neither cancerous nor cancer-free. They were "transitional." She still had to have three rounds of chemotherapy, but she knew in her heart that she was becoming cancer-free. Six years later, she is truly cancer-free. Even after both she and her ex-husband have moved on in their lives, she was able to tell him that she has forgiven him completely.

This is a true story of the power of the second chakra in our health. Without considering what motivated her anger and the tumor, Susie might never have been able to overcome the cancer. Susie is now a Healing Therapy practitioner whose goal in life is to help people heal.

Third Chakra – The Solar Plexus

The third chakra is one of personal power, where we develop our ego-self separate from our essence and inherited identity. This stage is where our defenses, or our "shell" gets built, still in the lower tier of our chakras.

Located in the solar plexus region of the body, its color is yellow. Yellow symbolizes courage, because to confront the challenges faced in this individuation requires "guts." It corresponds with. Wilbur's orange/yellow level of consciousness, which he calls "Multiplistic, Strive-Drive".'[31]

Illnesses originating here in such organs as stomach, pancreas, adrenals, upper intestines, gall bladder, and liver reflect our need for personal power and are related to issues of self-responsibility, self-esteem, fear of rejection, and oversensitivity to criticism.[32]

As we strengthen this core chakra with spiritual practices and learn to exercise our personal power for inner transformation, we will grow by leaps and bounds from the timid, fearful, self-preserving child to a confident, assertive and faithful person that God created us to be.

"Be all that you can be," might be the slogan for the third chakra, but self-esteem does not come without struggle, especially if we have never felt valued by those we love. Myss identifies four stages required in developing-self-esteem: *Revolution, Involution, Narcissism, and Evolution.*[33] No wonder adolescence is such a tormenting stage. Our first step is to revolt against the boundaries that have held us, and then, once we have left behind those boundaries, we wonder who we are left with and must examine and understand ourselves in a brand-new way. Self-knowledge is the beginning of wisdom, but on the way, we will have to go through the third stage of narcissism, where we create and revel in a new external image of what we have found inside. This sometimes takes courage, and it can be shocking to outsiders. When we have succeeded, we have evolved into an authentic person with the power to impact the world around us.

We will grow spiritually at this level as we learn to deal with success and failure and discover the real person we have hidden underneath our shell.

Fourth Chakra – The Heart

The fourth chakra consists of the heart and organs in the center of the chest. It is the transition level from Wilbur's first tier to the second. At this center of emotional energy, we develop relationships with others and ourselves at a higher spiritual level. Its color is green (sometimes pink), and it represents unconditional love for yourself and for others.

The heart is the life-center of the body and circulates our blood through our veins. Our sentient life is a gift of unconditional love from God. From this center, it is our task to accept that love and offer it freely to the world. At this a level of spiritual consciousness, we must have gone through the previous levels to purge ourselves of the need to be in control and to look good or even better than others. Wilbur refers to this classification of the heart chakra's level of consciousness is "pluralistic/conjunctive."[34]

With inflation in today's economy, many frightened people don't know how to heal their frustration and anger. Unattended, they can be depressed with no way to express it. If they have a genetic tendency toward cardiac problems, their body might experience heart artery blockages that become heart attacks. Recovery requires more than a self-help program. Good medical and/or psychological treatment would give them a much better chance to finally come to acceptance and forgiveness of their circumstance and be able to move on. A beloved spouse, a trustworthy spiritual director, or a counselor can make a spiritual difference that can heal. They could use a friend or therapist to help them work through their frustration. They could feel less alone, reminded of God's constant love and compassion.

Throughout our lives, emotions can confuse us and overwhelm us. Releasing our emotional pain is an important task for this energy center. Holding grudges, feeling rejected or unaccepted, and wanting revenge all deplete the energy of the heart. Resolution and forgiveness are the keyways that Divine energy can bring us back into this loving center. Coming to the point where we are ready to forgive (ourselves or the other) can come in incremental revelations of our value despite those hurts, but ultimately, we will learn to let go and give our wounds to God.

Injuries in the heart chakra—disappointment, rejection, betrayal—all require the ability to forgive, which is another way of saying to let go. But forgiveness does not come naturally. The solar plexus is not into forgiveness, but the heart is, when we are willing to use its energy's power.

This is the Time

O Divine Love,
This is the time
When my soul breaks open with longing.
Despair seeps through until you come.
You enter as an angel of peace.
You provide my punching bag.
You stand up to my doubts and fears.
As I pummel them into silence
You are all that is left.
Bigger than life, bigger than death,
You are my peace.

Fifth Chakra – The Throat

In the fifth chakra, located in the throat, we find the power of will in our lives. Our throat is our communication center, where we learn ultimately to surrender our willpower to the will of God. It is in the upper second tier because it is beginning to connect with God's will.

Most illnesses in our bodies are related to this center because it is our will or choice that is involved in every aspect of our lives. Specifically, however, illnesses of the thyroid, trachea, esophagus, throat, mouth, jaw and teeth are related to this energy center. Feelings of esteem or adequacy in the areas of communication of will constitute our personal power. Myss explains,

> The symbolic challenge of the Willpower Chakra is to progress through the maturation of will: from the tribal perception that everyone and everything around you has authority over you; through the perception that you alone have authority over you; to the final perception, that true authority comes from aligning yourself to *God's will*.[35]

In graduate school I took a course called, "Tavistock: Power and Authority in Task-Oriented Situations." It was an experiential group three-day exercise whose purpose was to develop leadership and managerial capacity to affect change in an organization.

What I witnessed in the course was a class full of people trying to exert their power over the decisions that had to be made. Success seemed to be judged on who had the most personal power.

I have typically avoided conflict or pain. As I participated in this class, I was only able to exert my will on the group through collaboration. I found that others in the group were not able to use collaboration, because it limited their personal power. In my paper for the course, I explained that the Tavistock method was not natural for me, and that I would rather deal with conflict in a more conciliatory way. It was a good insight for me, which held me in good stead for at least 20 years. However, there came a time that I had to deal with a personality conflict that needed a stronger presentation of my own will.

Wade in the Water

The power of a mighty stream
Will catch me in its flow,
Send me out into the depths –
Where it takes me, there I'll go.

Lift me up with buoyant waves
Beyond the crashing shore
Above the rocky, shallow edge
Where I will fear no more.

Spirit's gift keeps me on course,
My rescue and my rope,
My only line to pull me on
To calmer water's hope.

Spirit holds me close and dear,
God's loving heart I feel –
The pulse of new life in my soul
That comforts and will heal.

Trust is the key as I let go
Of fear and desperate need,
Past whirlpools' pull and rocky shoals
To Life in Spirit's lead.

I had founded a non-profit business with a board of individuals who brought with them a different vision from mine. When I was not able to present myself powerfully enough, I found I could not lead the organization toward my vision. I allowed my failure to tear at my self-esteem and my sense of purpose, which, I believe, eventually encompassed my throat and lower chakras in an unstable thyroid. This is an intuitive interpretation of the weakness that caused my illness, but to me, it explains the timing very well!

This conflict was fifth chakra dynamics in its most blatant form. Feeling loved and accepted is a precious gift. It comes more from a loving, open relationship between us and God. I wanted what I wanted so badly, I could not see into God's love and guidance at that moment. That others did not respect my vision was devastating. Be aware and learn that who you are is more than what people think of you!

The spiritual task of the fifth chakra is to unite my will with God's will.

As we progress in our spiritual journey (our relationship to God), we grow more open to the Spirit in all we do. This fifth spiritual stage and chakra, when combined with the wisdom gained from maturing through the previous stages, puts us in a place where we are more confident in our intuition and our need for Spirit to give us guidance and sustain us through conflict.

Sixth Chakra – The Mind

The mind is more mysterious to us than our will, for through it, we express and understand ourselves as the individuals we are. The "Ego-Aware" stage of spiritual consciousness delineated by Ken Wilbur corresponds with the mind chakra, in the third tier of our spiritual consciousness. There, we intellectually and consciously integrate all our autonomous as well as universal/divine aspects in the mind.

The color of the sixth chakra moves from light blue/turquoise to indigo.[36] Its center is in the middle of the forehead, but it connects throughout our body through the brain and neurological system, pituitary and pineal glands, ears, nose, and eyes.

Our mind gives us personal power to reason and evaluate. Sometimes called the "chakra of wisdom," we receive intuitive understandings here when our minds are receptive to Spirit's leadings. This is why in some cultures the sixth chakra is called the "third eye." Wilbur explains that as we grow in this level of consciousness, we learn to detach from what might be called the "beginners mind" (literal/magical) and relate to the power and insight of the open or "impersonal mind"[37] (logical).

Mental illness comes when the mind is overwhelmed with the details of living, when our personal pieces of facts, fears, personal experiences and memories don't fit together or make sense. Often, life doesn't make sense, even when we have a healthy mind. We throw out our perspective as a net over all we come into contact with. We can only see what we know, and that leads to confusion, conflict and frustration in our minds. The spiritual task of detachment opens those crowded, confused thoughts to another perspective – God's.

The question then becomes spiritual: "Where is God in all this?" Maybe the more important question is: "How is my perspective different from God's?" Growth in detachment can lead to enlightened attitudes and openness to healing and revelation.

To detach is to objectively review the content of our minds and emotional data. When we become more conscious of our incongruencies, we become emotionally congruent in what we think and do. From the Christian perspective, it is here that we learn to be Christ's disciples, or the Body of Christ.

Healing requires a unity of heart and mind when we can recognize how our feelings are influencing our thoughts. Our thoughts do influence our health. Fears and stresses pull us away from our center and block out the life-giving Spirit from our recovery. When open and receptive, the mind can help us heal.

Many therapists recommend affirmations as the key to health, because by using them we reinforce good thoughts of ourselves. "I am strong and confident, and can face this situation," is a good affirmation. I think this is borne out of scripture, which is even more basic to our mind's health:

Rejoice in the Lord always. I will say it again: Rejoice! Let your gentleness be evident to all. The Lord is near. Do not be anxious about anything, but in everything, by prayer and petition, with thanksgiving, present your requests to God. And *the peace of God, which transcends all understanding*, will guard your hearts and your minds in Christ Jesus.

Finally brothers, whatever is true, whatever is noble, whatever is right, whatever is pure, whatever is lovely, whatever is admirable — if anything is excellent or praiseworthy — think about such things. Whatever you have learned or received or heard from me, or seen in me — put it into practice. And the God of peace will be with you. [38]

We do fill our minds with destructive thoughts that separate us from God. We watch television shows and movies that dwell on revenge and conflict; we play video games where we are the great villain. We plot to get the best advantage over others, and we'll do anything to get it. It's easy to degrade our thoughts into our lower chakras to seek personal power and security until we can't see what God sees: A beautiful, beloved creation who has lost the way and needs to find the way back.

The bigger picture of the sixth chakra is God's vision of peace, harmony and balance, love, acceptance—all wrapped in the cloak of unity and openness to the Spirit that gives us life.

Thomas Merton, the 20th century Christian mystic, wrote, "There is in all things a hidden wholeness." The less integrated our lives are—the less we can see the whole—the more broken we become.

The psalmist also knew the breadth of the Spirit:

Where can I go from your Spirit ?
Where can I flee from your presence?
If I go up to the heavens, you are there;
if I make my bed in the depths, you are there.
If I rise on the wings of the dawn,
if I settle on the far side of the sea,
even there your hand will guide me,
your right hand will hold me fast.

If I say, "Surely the darkness will hide me
and the light become night around me,"
even the darkness will not be dark to you;
the night will shine like the day,
for darkness is as light to you.

How precious to me are your thoughts, O God!
How vast is the sum of them!
Were I to count them[39]

Seventh Chakra – The Crown

The seventh chakra is our spiritual connector, in which our spirit is completely integrated, where Divine guidance is continually received. At the top of Tier 3, its body location is at the crown of the head, where the Spirit/Breath of Life can enter and energize and nourish our whole bodies. It represents our highest connection to the transcendent and transpersonal dimension of life, both in the chakra system and in Wilbur's integrated spirituality system. Its color progresses from violet to white. Its energy influences the central nervous system, the muscular system and the skin. It generates devotion, inspirational and prophetic thoughts, transcendent ideas and mystical connections.[40]

Seventh chakra spiritual energy can be called "the grace of God," where all good gifts originate. Faith and fear can dwell in this place of union with God, whether we experience spiritual highs or dark nights of the soul. As we consciously grow to operate from this level, we live our lives in the intimate company of the Divine. Prayer in this level is not supplication, but instead, it is rest in the Presence. No words are necessary. It is a "knowing" and a companionship.

We prepare ourselves for this stage of spiritual awareness by our studies of sacred texts, time spent in prayer, and activities done for the fulfillment of God's purpose in our lives. No one begins here, some have moments here, but few can function here continually.

Mother Theresa confided to her spiritual director that she had not felt the presence of God with her for years, and sometimes this was a source of pain and doubt. Her experience was the classic "Dark Night of the

Soul," a period when she had to do her ministry and live her life without continual emotional assurances of God's presence. Her strength was in her *greater consciousness* (Stage 7), her grounded faith that God was with her no matter how alone she felt. This is a seventh chakra experience, one that, during turmoil, can sustain a person to question her feelings and yet be strengthened in her faith by knowing without feeling.

We all come to impasses in our lives where we ask, "Where is God?" But when we are at this violet level of spiritual consciousness, we know that it is only our senses that are dull, and God is always with us.

Reaching the seventh chakra of spiritual consciousness can only come from letting go and allowing God to work through us and in us. When we learn to meditate or do contemplation, we are opening our soul to the point where our ego-selves are no longer in control.

Jesus, as human as he was Divine, exemplifies this stage of spiritual consciousness. He lived in connection to God through Spirit, and he sought out the disciplines of the spirit to keep this connection. He went up on the mountain to pray because he had to take time to get away from the crowds and center himself in God's love. He taught things that seemed strange even to the disciples. "You have heard that it was said, 'Eye for eye, and tooth for tooth.' But I tell you, do not resist an evil person. If someone strikes you on the right cheek, turn to him the other also." [41] Jesus had mercy on people who were outcasts, and he healed them.

At this spiritual stage, you begin to see the world through God's eyes, and you will be transformed. You will truly become a "new creation." This is not a stage for wimps. People who live in open union with God will seem different enough to become alienated from society, condemned, and even assassinated. They float along the razor's edge without touching it, buoyed by the Spirit, knowing that they will risk their lives for union with God.

Practice and Ideas to Ponder

1. Journal about your experience living in each of the stages of spiritual consciousness.

   a. Tribal
   b. Life in Relationship
   c. Ego-Centered Self-Esteem
   d. Unconditional love
   e. Aligned with the Will of God
   f. Detachment
   g. Union with God

2. Think about a person whose political views are opposite of yours. What can you do to accept that person as a child of God and love them as God does?

   a. Write out your perspective.
   b. Try to see their perspective.
   c. Look for God's perspective.

3. For group discussion: Jake was just laid off from his career job of 30 years. He never would have wanted to leave this job because he had been so proud to work for the company. Even with a lay-off package, he was mad at the company: he felt unappreciated and worthless, and they didn't seem to care about his future or his family. He was scared and depressed. Jake couldn't move on because of his fear and anger. He was suffering from depression and digestive problems. His wife, Jane, tried to offer him support, but he was too depressed to do something about it so that he could find a job and get on with his life. What are three things that Jane could do if she understood which of his chakras were affected?

4. What spiritual stage do you spend most of your waking hours in? Why?

5. Do you know any people in our modern world who live primarily in the seventh spiritual stage? Do you think that is possible? Why or why not?

CHAPTER 7

Living as God's Child

*...For it is God who works in you to will and
to act according to his good purpose.*

Phil 2:13 NIV

Set Afire in Faith

Abba Lot said to the wise old Joseph, "Abba, as far as I can, I say my little office, I fast a little, I pray and meditate, I live in peace, and as far as I can, I purify my thoughts. What else can I do?" Abba Joseph rose and stretched his hands toward heaven. His fingers were like ten lamps of fire as he responded: "If you will, you can become all flame."[42]

What would it take to become "all flame?" What would light me up from the inside out and set me to doing and being all that God made me to be? Our little prayer practices may seem small, but when we are filled with Spirit, we do glow from the inside. But what about the outside? Most of us know that the peace we find in meditation is sometimes lost when we leave our space and go to confront our world. Is Spirit "either/or?" We can pretend it is that way, but some wise souls know that it is "all-in-one."

Grow and Glow

Dear God,
Thank you for all that grows and glows with your essence.
Thank you for being, for creating who I am.

May I grow and glow
With your essence
Of Wisdom and Light,
May all I do and say
Reflect only you,
Harmony and Peace.

May all Creation emanate you
In friends, flowers, weeds and trees.
In sunshine, moonlight,
Darkness and sleep.

May we find unity in your love
ONE in deep connection
ONE in creative fecundity
As life gives and dies
And releases newness every morning.
To grow and glow
Felt and known among us.
Amen.

LIVING AS GOD'S CHILD

We may be blessed with times that we feel filled with Spirit. In the Christian tradition, we describe it as Holy Spirit. Experiences in Cursillo and Walk to Emmaus retreat weekends enable such a communion: Mountaintop experiences for the individual in community with others who are praying together and completely rely on the power of the Holy Spirit to work in them for renewal, revelation and joy. The prayer for the Holy Spirit which is interlaced throughout the retreat is a shared call for this power: "Come, Holy Spirit. Fill the hearts of your faithful and kindle in us the fire of your love. Send forth your Spirit that we may be created, and you shall renew the face of the earth...."

Kathleen Morris, in her essay titled, "The Quotidian Mysteries," talks about growing our spirituality through the monotonous little activities of our lives—laundry, liturgy and "Women's Work." [43] It is true, we undervalue those everyday tasks, thinking that they make no difference in our lives. But Spirit is not just for mountaintop times. It is for every day, every minute, every activity. A person who is dissatisfied with the everyday mundane life because they want to always feel the mountaintop will soon find that their addiction to the mountaintop is a false spirituality. Spirituality must be grounded in everyday life.

Brother Lawrence was an 18th century Carmelite lay brother living in a monastery. At first, Brother Lawrence felt his menial work in the monastery kitchen kept him from his prayers. It was boring, and it wasn't "spiritual." Eventually, he discovered something during that enforced time of "meaningless" work. God was there with him, and he could be with God – talk, praise, listen and learn—even in those seemingly trivial chores like peeling potatoes. He said he concentrated on doing little things for God, since he was unable to do bigger things.[44]

He began his practice by cultivating a deep presence of God in his heart. He said that God's presence had to be maintained by the heart and by love rather than by understanding and speech.[45]

> "The most effective way Brother Lawrence had for communicating with God was to simply do his ordinary work. He did this obediently, out of a pure love of God, purifying it as much as was humanly possible. He believed it was a serious mistake to think of our prayer

time as being different from any other. Our actions should unite us with God when we are involved in our daily activities, just as our prayers unite us with him in our quiet devotions."[46]

Washing dishes, doing laundry, walking, gardening—every little activity is an opportunity to enjoy the company of God's Spirit who journeys with us through every moment of every day. What a revelation. Many people think that they have to say a formal prayer to talk to God. Formal prayer is good in community settings. But since the Spirit of God is our closest friend, why not treat Spirit as a friend with whom we walk and talk and work in every moment? Activity with God is no longer monotonous. It will bring us joy and release. You are never alone.

I hope you see the signs of what could be called a seventh stage of spirituality in Brother Lawrence. He opened his soul in union with God in all he did. To live in that stage requires self-discipline and letting go – a paradox if there ever was one.

Perhaps none of us is at this spiritual level, but we can grow toward it. When we think of connection with God as a task that must be performed, it is easy for our devotion to God to become boring, tedious, or something we'd rather not do. If some days our prayer seems to be nothing more than a repetition of meaningless words, instead of beating ourselves up over not being good enough, we simply ask God to help us long to be in God's presence all the time.

The monastics through the centuries can teach us about this problem. Third- and fourth-century desert monks, the Abbas and the Ammas, called this condition *acedia*, when their lives slowed down into an unrelenting test of endurance for the mundane spiritual tasks they promised to perform. I believe the source of acedia is in our trying to "do it right," instead of simply trusting and waiting for the peaceful and encouraging company of the Spirit.

Amid all the technology and conveniences of life in the 21st Century, we find no delight in God unless it is on our terms. Our everyday life can seem meaningless. Little things mean nothing, and we just don't care to go on doing them. It's the torpor of sitting in your big chair mindlessly flipping the remote for the TV. This is not depression, which is a deeper withdrawal and more obvious. Instead, acedia is insidious to our boredom, self-centeredness and disconnection with Spirit working in our lives. How ironic that it was first noticed among those monks who especially sought after Spirit's guidance.

Thomas Aquinas makes a distinction between acedia and despair. "For despair, participation in the divine nature through grace is perceived as appealing, but impossible; for acedia, the prospect is possible, but unappealing.[47] It makes me think of Albert Camus' philosophy: *ça ne fait rien*. (It doesn't matter.) What does matter? What is getting in the way?

Whatever its source, acedia can be cast out by prayer and sustaining songs/words. Leave no room for the spirit of acedia. Fill your mind with thoughts that will uplift you, teach you and encourage you. Do what needs to be done, and then rest in Spirit's provisions. Have you ever wondered why a tune or a song goes through your head? Look carefully at the words your mind/subconscious is saying. They could lead you to where your mind needs to go. Sometimes they can be little jokes – a silly song that means to lighten you up or take you to a happier thought. Just notice. Then, be thankful.

The very repetitions that seem so monotonous can be lifesaving. They are prayer when you feel no prayer within your heart. Time spent folding the laundry, doing dishes, making beds provide a special time for you with Spirit.

Benedictine communities pray the Psalms every day, so that they might call upon those words whenever they are needed. The Psalms are the human cry for God in our most dry or tormented circumstances. In Psalm 22:1, King David wrote, "My God, My God, why have you forsaken me?" Jesus knew those words in his heart and was able to repeat them as he hung on the cross.

Memory verses, poems and psalms that have deep meaning come to me when I don't really have words to pray, but I seek out Spirit for sustenance. One of my favorites is the Good News Bible version of Psalm 16:5-6. When I first read that version, I memorized it immediately so that I could carry it with me wherever I went: *You, Lord, are all I have. You give me all I need. My future is in your hands. How wonderful are your gifts to me. How good they are!*

When I say those encouraging words during a time of worry about what is happening in my life, they bring a deep comfort. I affirm that I trust God implicitly, and I recognize God's presence. I am led to think positive thoughts about what God has done for me in the past. I know that I am capable and loved. What happens next is no longer a subject for my worry, but a subject for trust. Many psalms can do the same thing for you if they speak what you have really been feeling.

Jesus counseled his disciples about the death that he faced. He gave them these comforting words: "Peace I leave with you; my peace I give you. I do not give to you as the world gives. Do not let your hearts be troubled and do not be afraid."[48]

Jesus modeled the deep connection with God that helps us find peace and comfort, courage and determination. Prayer is an expression of that connection, whether it be in the form of requests, thanksgiving, silence in God's presence, or simply placing our fears in trust with God. Prayer groups can be helpful in developing that connection, as, with the support of other like-minded individuals, a person can practice trusting in Spirit's presence. When that learning becomes a part of who we are, we are on the path of a life lived in the wholeness that God wants for us.

How we think prayer should be is a good indicator of the stage of spirituality that we dwell in.

- A first chakra prayer would be to serve the interests of the tribe/family in warfare or wealth by asking for favor with God.
- A second chakra prayer would ask for special favors that serve my interests and my standing in the community.
- A third chakra prayer would ask for personal favor with God, for power and influence.
- A fourth chakra prayer would seek God's love and comfort, both for me and for others, and I would return that love in my praise. Intercessory prayer comes from the heart.
- A fifth chakra prayer would ask what God's will is for me.
- A sixth chakra prayer would ask God to teach me how to live so that I might love others as much as I love myself and God.
- A seventh chakra prayer would open my spirit to be transformed into God's likeness.

Prayer as Energy

Jesus is the great healer. During his life on earth, his consciousness was completely aligned with God's will. We do not know all the ways that conscious connection with God works, but with the understanding of energy work, we know we have the same abilities to do what he did to heal people. Even Jesus told us that.

> I tell you the truth, anyone who has faith in me will do what I have been doing. He will do even greater things than these, because I am going to the Father. And I will do whatever you ask in my name, so that the Son may bring glory to the Father. You may ask me for anything in my name, and I will do it.[49]

Our prayers express our conscious communication and link with God. New studies teach us that thoughts have energy. Intention is a thought. When we meditate, we intend to be entirely present to God. When the energy practitioner practices healing therapy, the intention of the mind must be completely on loving and bringing wholeness and healing to the person treated. The energy does not only flow through the hands, but from the mind. Dr. Polkinghorne has explained this through his scientific vision:

> When we pray, we are seeking for a laser-like coherence between our will and God's This has two consequences. One is that prayer is not a substitute for action, rather, it is a necessary component of action.... We feel that it is a good thing to have many people praying for the same cause. What is the force of this? More fists beating on the heavenly door and so more likely to attract the divine attention? I think not. However, more wills being aligned with the divine will, and therefore, greater power at work in the divine-human collaboration that is the act of petitionary prayer; this is what we are doing when we pray together.[50]

When our wills are aligned with divine will, prayer is very powerful. When we participate in prayer chains or other extended prayer groups, we are aligning our wills for the greater good of someone prayed for. The reason some prayers do not get the results we are asking for has more to do with opening our will to God's rather than telling God what should be done.

One example of how this worked was when the Berlin Wall came down in 1989. It seemed such a surprise to the general population of the world that this could happen. But it was no surprise to the millions of prayers that a particular prayer campaign had instigated in the weeks before for that wall to come down. God is great, and with our intentions aligned with God's, miracles can happen!

On a more intimate level, I was in a hospital room as pastor with a dying man's family. Jake could no longer speak because he was considered brain-dead. He would be gone soon. I asked them to join hands all around him to pray. I could feel their love as we joined hands and prayed that Jake would feel God's power within him and all of us would know that Jake was in God's care. As I said the word *Power*, his body jerked, and he cried out. It startled everyone, thinking he couldn't possibly respond in any way. Later, after the family left, I came back to the room to talk to his wife. She was joyous to tell me that she had fallen asleep in the chair and had dreamed that she had had a conversation with Jake on a cloud. He told her that he had to go now, but that he loved her so much and wanted to say goodbye. What a gift God had given her through prayer! He died a few days later.

Let us not become so entranced with the power Spirit provides through prayer to think that *we* can cure anything. Our finite understanding reveals so little of God's plan, and in humility we must know that some disabilities – genetic or accident-caused – are to be accepted as part of our life and part of the creation we live in. Scientific studies will continue to develop new paths to healing. Perhaps miracle healings will occur from our prayers. But we are not the ones to decide when that will happen.

Understand Your Gifts

Many churches provide spiritual gift inventories to help members discover what unique gifts God has given to us for service and for love in the world. Several are online that could help determine your major strengths. A spiritual gift is different from talent. Talents are things that come easily to us and help us determine what we do (perform) best. If we are talented at singing, with experience and training, we might want to become a professional singer.

On the other hand, a spiritual gift may not come easy to us right away, but God may place a desire in us that leads us to want to do something for the special good of God's world. With perseverance, education, practice and dedication, these gifts form the basis of how we demonstrate God's spirit in our everyday lives. Many spiritual gifts are talents, but their spirituality resides in our motivation to use them. I may have a talent in music because I sing or play an instrument well. What makes it spiritual is how it conveys God's grace to people I sing or play for.

The Apostle Paul has provided us with several lists of spiritual gifts, and I believe there are more than those, because God can help us pass on God's grace in everything we do. Here is Paul's list from his First Letter to the Corinthians:

> Now to each one the manifestation of the Spirit is given for the common good. To one there is given through the Spirit the message of wisdom, to another the message of knowledge by means of the same Spirit, to another faith by the same Spirit, to another gifts of healing by that one Spirit, to another miraculous powers, to another prophecy, to another distinguishing between spirits, to another speaking in different kinds of tongues, and to still another the interpretation of tongues. All these are the work of one and the same Spirit, and he gives them to each one, just as he determines.[51]

Wisdom, knowledge, faith, healing, performing miracles, apostleship, prophecy, discerning of spirits and speaking in tongues are a good beginning for gifts that make us ministers to others. Modern lists also include helping, music, praying, administration, evangelism, missionary, exhortation, faith, giving, hospitality, intercession, mercy, leadership, service, shepherd, teaching, and voluntary poverty. You may take the inventory online to find out what your primary spiritual gifts are.[52]

Your spiritual gifts today may be very different from what they were ten years ago or even ten years from now. You are growing into the person God created you to be. You are who you were meant to be at each stage. Appreciate where you are and who you are.

When I was 20, the last thing I thought I would be was a healer. I was giddy, ungrounded, silly and very distracted. I didn't even know what my major in college should be because I liked to do so many things. God was working in me. Forty years later, Spirit led me into healing ministry. I am amazed!

Let God amaze you at what you can do and be. Pray for guidance and openness for all that is to come. But remember, the journey lasts a lifetime.

Examine Your Circumstances in the Light of Your Gifts

Sometimes we make excuses for not allowing ourselves to grow. First, it's more comfortable to stay right where we are. As long as nothing changes, life is easy, and I'm happy. The problem is, something always changes, whether you instigate it or not, good or bad, you will experience change. Life is like a wave on the sea with its ups and downs and roll-overs. Your existence is meant to be turned and prodded, expanded and shrunk into something new. Your hope is in your relationship with God, the Spirit, who will sustain you.

> "Because of the LORD's great love we are not consumed,
> for his compassions never fail.
> They are new every morning;
> great is your faithfulness.
> I say to myself, "The LORD is my portion;
> therefore I will wait for him."[53]

So go ahead and try something new, even scary. If someone needs something from you, do it for them out of love. Study and learn, practice, grow and stretch until somebody can feel God's touch through you.

The secretary, the administrator, the janitor, the CEO, the clerk at the supermarket—any who seek a spiritual connection with God—have spiritual gifts that you can recognize and give thanks for.

Live as God's Child

Life as God's child might feel like a bucketful of challenges. Yes, there have to be challenges for you to grow as God's child, but with the help from Spirit for the journey, you will meet them and overcome them. About 12 years ago, I had a deep realization that the younger generations are seeking spiritual help but have no grounding for their search. I wanted to help them as a spiritual director. I decided to call myself "Spiritseeker," just as we all are. When I enrolled a Farm in Farm Town on Facebook, my avatar was named "Spiritseeker." That personna described my mission in life at this stage.

To my surprise, it resulted in a strange experience with my avatar on Farm Town. I went to the cyber-market to hire harvesters, and I hired a young man from England, probably no more than 16. As he harvested the crops on my farm, he wrote/asked me a question: "Do you see spirits?"

I hadn't thought that my avatar's name would bring that connection, but I told him, "No, I'm a pastor wanting to help people connect with the Spirit of God." He wanted to talk to me about his mother who had passed and wanted to know if she was with him. We had a good conversation on the computer, and I was glad that my avatar's name was Spiritseeker.

Dealing with the loss of a loved one makes one search for grounding. We have a universal need to feel God within us, even if, intellectually, we want to reject the notion. My ministry in this life is to share the good news that Spirit is with us every moment of every day, and we can intentionally grow up as God's child. Our focus is changed from fears that we will not be good enough or be liked into recognizing who we are in God's eyes and how loved we are.

What difference does that make in your life? You will be changed. You will grow in love, joy, peace, patience, kindness, goodness, faithfulness, gentleness and self-control – all the fruit of the Spirit.[54] God will re-form you into a new person with a new hope for a new life. We can truly love our lives and the people who fill it because of this Spirit. We will act out of a spirit of confidence and optimism that we do not go alone.

A New Hope

Dark the night of wait and wonder,
Heavy mystery cloaks the skies.
Weary, watching, searching ever
For the light of God's surprise.

Fog of cloud and dew of cover
Gently move on breath of air.
Parting slowly, leave their hover,
Stars of light and hope to bear.

A new hope for a new day ... in a new life!

Rising light, its presence growing
As the star appears in view --
Shimmers brightly, dances, glowing
Points the way for me and you.

Light now penetrates the heaven
Warming cold and frozen hearts,
Piercing joy for new life given,
God is with us, sadness parts!

A new hope for a new day ... in a new life!

Second Timothy reminds us again to become aflame in the Spirit: "This is why I remind you to fan into flames the spiritual gifts God gave you when I laid my hands on you. For God has not given us a spirit of fear and timidity, but of power, of love and of self-discipline."[55]

When I see myself as God sees me, I am whole and perfect, released from the grip of my ego. I choose to focus on all that is good, health-full and enriching. This will keep me moving forward so that I can grow into full maturity in Spirit. I will be aware of all my blessings and take responsibility for being a blessing to others. Life in the Spirit will make my life full and joyful, whole and full of possibilities.

Practice and Ideas to Ponder

1. Use this poem to begin a meditation period.

Breath of Life

Breathe in God's gift of life.
Breathe in and out.
Breathe deeply.
Let God's breath enliven you
with spirit
with energy,
with peace.
Let your mind rest on that breath.
Let your muscles ride on that breath.
As it moves gently through you,
Be cleansed of your dingy,
dark and musty corners.
Be swept clean of the tight, cluttered places
Where hurts and hatred harbor.
Float in its buoyancy
Fly under its current
Be made new by its grace.
The breath swells from within,
pressing for release.
You can't contain it.
Inside you are re-formed
And your breath
Is *trans*formed with Spirit's power.
Let it out on word and song in air—
Sing through it songs of joy
Speak through it words of love
Fill the air around you with grace.
The world is different because of your breath
enriching your space.
Through you, God is real.
You are a sign of God's life in the world.

2. What are some of your favorite words of encouragement? If you don't have one, search through the book of Psalms, highlighting text that speaks to you. Look further, into Proverbs or Lamentations. Particularly powerful are Proverbs 3:5 and Lamentations 3:22.

3. Take the time to take the Spiritual Gifts Inventory online if you haven't done it before: http://buildingchurch.net/g2s.htm. How do you express your spiritual gifts in your home, where you work and where you worship?

4. Think about the people you interact with at church, at the store or the place you work. If you truly notice them, can you see a spiritual gift making an appearance? If they don't have one that is obvious to you, pray for them to grow into one. Give thanks for Spirit's presence through others in your life.

5. Make a list of lifestyle changes that you would like to incorporate into your life for wholeness in the Spirit.

About the Author

Healing and wholeness inspire Mary Edlund's passion for ministry: To assist those who seek to grow in spiritual understanding of God's role in their life, regardless of their religious affiliation. A spiritual director, small group leader, retreat leader and Healing (energy) Therapist, Mary is a retired Full Deacon in the United Methodist Church, having served in conference and parish ministry as well as wholeness ministry. Her spiritual direction training was from the Hesychia School of Spiritual Direction in Tucson, Arizona.

Several of her devotional poems have been published as choral anthems composed by Eugene Butler. Other poems are included in this book. Theological studies from various seminaries and a master's degree in mass communications from the University of Minnesota prepared her for service as Steward of Communications for the Minnesota Annual Conference United Methodist Church before moving to Durango, Colorado in 2001.

Mary enjoys inventing characters for fantasy adventures, and she has honed her skills in writing children's stories and poems as well as movie and television scripts for children as she reared her two daughters, Erin and Alison. She and her husband, Lee, live in the Denver, Colorado, area and enjoy the blessings of a granddaughter, Autumn.

Resources

Andrew Weil, Sounds True Beta. (1999). Breathing: The Master Key to Self-Healing. Boulder, CO, United States of America.

Howell, K. (Composer). (2002). Sacred Ground: Music and Window Frequencies for Meditation. [Brain Sync Corporation, Performer] Santa Fe, New Mexico, United States of America.

Short form free enneagram test. (n.d.). Retrieved 2010, from http://www.karunacounseling.com/enneagram.htm

Long form Enneagram Inventory $10. (n.d.). Retrieved 2010, from http://wwweneagraminstitute.com

Bibliography

Daniels, David, M. D. (2000). *The Essential Enneagram: The Definitive Personaliity Test and Self-Discovery Guide.* New York, NY: Harper One/ Harper Collins.

Davis, J. *A Word from "Brother" Jeanne.* Pageturner, Press and Media, 2019.

Ebert, R. R. (2006). *The Enneagram: A Christian Perspective.* New York, NY: Crossroad Publishing Company.

Hoerth, P. (March, 2010). Sustainability and Spiritual Direction. *Presence, an International Journal of Spiritual Direction,* 13-19.

Hover-Kramer, D. (2002). *Healing Touch: A Guidebook for Practitioners.* Albany, NY: Delmar, a division of Thomson Learning, Inc.

Kathleen Deignan, Ed. Forward by James Finley, Illustrations by John Giuliani. (2007). *Thomas Merton: A Book of Hours.* Notre Dame, Indiana: Sorin Books.

Lawrence, B. (1982). *The Practice of the Presence of God.* New Kensington, PA: Whitaker House.

Mathis, Rick P. (2000). *Prayer-Centered Healing: Finding the God Who Heals.* Liguori, Missouri: Liguori.

Myss, Caroline (1999). *Anatomy of the Spirit.* New York, NY: Three Rivers Press.

Myss, C. (2003). *Sacred Contracts, Awakening Your Divine Potential.* New York, NY: Three Rivers Press.

Norris, K. (2008). *Acedia and me: A Marriage, Monks, and A Writer's Life.* New York, NY: The Penguin Group.

Norris, K. (1998) *The Quotidien Mysteries: Laundry, Liturgy and "Women's Work,"* New York, NY: Paulist Press.

Norrisey, C. P. (1991). *Prayer and Temperament, Different Prayer Forms for Different Personality Types.* Charlottesville, VA: The Open Door, Inc.

Palmer, H. (1983). *The Enneagram: Understanding Yourself and the Others in Your Life.* New York, NY: HarperCollins Publishers.

Palmer, P. (2004). *A Hidden Wholeness.* Hoboken, NJ: A Wiley Imprint.

Polkinghorne, J. (1994). *Quarks, Chaos & Christianity.* New York, NY: Crossroad.

Riso, D. R. (1995). *Discovering Your Personality Type.* New York, NY: Houghton Mifflin.

Wilbur, K. (2006). *Integral Spirituality, A Startling New Role for Religion in the Modern and Postmodern World.* Boston and London: Integral Books.

Endnotes

1. Palmer, H., **The Enneagram**, p. 17
2. Rohr, Richard and Andreas Ebert, **The Enneagram: A Christian Perspective,** p. 245.
3. Rohr, Richard and Andreas Ebert , Ibid. p. 294
4. Michael, Chester P. and Norrisey, Marie C., **Prayer and Temperament, Different Prayer Forms for Different Personality Types**. Chapter 2.
5. Ibid., pp. 11-20
6. John 14:12-13 NIV
7. John 17: 22 – 23 NIV
8. Davis, Jeanne Webb, **A Word from "Brother" Jeanne,** (unpublished), p. 26.
9. Myss, Caroline, **Sacred Contracts**
10. Merton, Thomas, **A Book of Hours**, p. 62
11. Palmer, Parker, **A Hidden Wholeness**, pages 46- 47.
12. Hover-Kramer, Dorothea, **Healing Touch, A Guidebook for Practitioners,** p. 71.
13. Polkinghorne, John**, Quarks, Chaos & Christianity**, pp. 55-56.
14. Ps 139:13-16 NIV
15. Middleton, Carl Ph.D., **Healing Therapy Manual,** Catholic Health Initiatives. Denver, CO. 2004.
16. Norris, Kathleen, **Acedia and me**, **A Marriage, Monks, and A Writer's Life**, p. 141

17 Mathis, Rick, Ph.D., **Prayer-Centered Healing: Finding the God Who Heals,** p. 48
18 Luke 10:28 NIV
19 Howell, Kelly *Sacred Ground* (CD)
20 "Sustainability and Spiritual Direction," Pat Hoerth, P**resence, an International Journal of Spiritual Direction**, Vol. 6, No. 1, March 2010, page 17
21 Myss, Caroline **Anatomy of the Spirit.** (Norris, 2008) (Norris) (Norris)Note: There are actually eight energy centers, but the eighth is above the head and identified as "transpersonal."
22 Dorothea Hover-Kramer, **Healing Touch, A Guidebook for Practitioners**, 2nd Ed., p. 65
23 Wilbur, Ken op.cit., p. 90.
24 Ibid, pages 68-69
25 Myss, Caroline op.cit., page 104
26 Ibid, page 110.
27 Wilbur, Ken, op.cit., pages 68-69
28 Myss Caroline, op.cit.., page 132
29 Ibid, pages 133, 134
30 Ibid, page132
31 Ibid
32 Myss, Caroline op. cit., page 167.
33 Ibid, pages 187-192
34 Wilbur, Ken, op. cit., page 68-69.
35 Myss, Carol (Norris, The Quotidien Mysteries--Laundry, Liturgy and 'Women's Work' , 1998), op.cit., page 219.
36 Wilbur, Ken, op. cit., pages 68-69.
37 Ibid, page 238
38 Philippians 4: 4-9 NIV
39 Psalm 139:7-12, 17-18.
40 Myss, Caroline op.cit., p. 265
41 Matt. 5:38-39 NIV
42 Norris, Kathleen op.cit., p. 134
43 Norris, Kathleen **The Quotidien Mysteries—Laundry, Liturgy and 'Women's Work.**
44 Lawrence, Brother, **The Practice of the Presence of God,** p.18.

45 Ibid, p. 80
46 Ibid, p. 24.
47 Ibid, p. 24.
48 John 14:28 NIV
49 John 14:12-14 NIV
50 Ibid, pp. 75-76
51 1 Cor 12:7-11 NIV (Other biblical references include Romans 12:3-8, Corinthians 14:1-40, Ephesians 4:7-16, and 1 Peter 4:7-11.)
52 http://buildingchurch.net/g2s-i.htm
53 Lam 3:22-24 NIV
54 Galatians 5:22-23 NIV
55 2 Tim 1:6-7 NLT

www.ingramcontent.com/pod-product-compliance
Lightning Source LLC
LaVergne TN
LVHW091535070526
838199LV00001B/74